The life and Clinic of a psychotherapist

ROSA CUKIER

Introduction

This book consists of eight articles that were written and published in specialized journals over the last 10 years. At first sight, they are different articles that discuss various themes. However, after reading them in more depth, you will notice that they all revolve around the theme of child abuse and its consequences for the psychodynamics of adult clients.

I have always felt mobilized to study issues related to early childhood, especially child abuse and the indelible marks it leaves on the psyche. Domestic violence, narcissistic and borderline disorders, brain function - I am under the impression that I have always studied the same thing from different points of view, and I have always wanted to use and teach how to apply psychodrama to treat resulting conditions.

The articles will be presented in the chronological order in which I wrote them. I will share with you the context of my personal life, in which the curiosity and desire to write them was awakened. The first article, *"Codependency"*, was written in popular language for a neighborhood newsletter around 1996-1997. At that time, I was in psychotherapy, and I was personally very interested in the issues surrounding child abuse and its consequences in adult life. I asked my therapist who was also my teacher, Dr. Dalmiro Bustos, for bibliographical suggestions, and he referred me to Alice Miller's book *The Drama of the Gifted Child* (1997).

This book changed my way of looking at psychopathology and led to me reading several correlated texts, including that of a North American author called John Bradshaw with whom I did a workshop in the United States of America (USA).

It was there that I heard the term "codependency" for the first time and learnt about Melody Beattie's book, *Codependent No More* (1998). This is an interesting term as codependency refers to mutual dependence: someone trying to control an addiction or their own dysfunctional behavior –depression, for example – and another person, usually someone in the family, totally dependent on his/her success or failure. This is perhaps the term that best describes the attachment-related psychodynamics in dysfunctional families.

I wrote the second article, *"Therapist fatigue: secondary post-traumatic stress"*, in 2002. I was motivated by personal fatigue, professional weariness, and a desire to slow down. I had published three books in the last 10 years, I worked in a clinic giving group and individual therapy and I was often invited to run workshops in São Paulo and in other places. I began to realize that I did not want to have messages waiting for me on my answering machine – I preferred it when there were fewer patients on my schedule – and had recently been diagnosed with fibromyalgia; in short, I was not okay.

I found the term "burnout" on the Internet and ordered some books from Amazon as there was not much literature on the subject in Brazil. It turned out to be a research project that lasted about 2 years, which resulted in a decrease in my workload and an increase in the light blue colored spaces in my schedule. That was my secret code for pool and swimming, a physical activity that helped me enormously in recovering from this condition.

"The Psychodrama of Mankind: Is it really Utopian?", the third article, was also written in 2002. It was August, 1998 and I had just published my second book (on issues related to power abuse, domestic violence and psychological disorders and their resulting narcissists) and had already started researching my third book (vocabulary of quotations from the entire work of Jacob Levi Moreno), when I attended the 13th International Congress of Group Psychotherapy in London.

I had already been to other International Congresses and felt pleasantly curious, kitted out with a notebook and open to new ideas. The first or second plenary of the Congress was given by Vamik Volkan (1997), an Emeritus Professor of Psychiatry at the University of Virginia (USA), who is of Turkish Cypriot origin. He had just published a book called Bloodlines and his talk left me speechless.

What Volkan asserted, in front of an audience full of human behavior scholars and researchers, resonated with me both concerning Moreno's work – which I was already analyzing and reading in detail – and my second book including the pertinent issues surrounding narcissism I mentioned in it. Basically, he said that large groups, when wounded in their pride and ideology, seek to retaliate, and take revenge, just like children who, emotionally abused during childhood, seek, as adults, an active attitude of revenge for their wounded dignity.

Moreno had always wanted to use psychodrama to heal humanity, and Vamik Volkan seemed to show the necessity and current relevance of Moreno´s intention. So, I took several notes, left the lecture and bought the book. I started reading the book while still at the hotel and could not put it down. The article that follows is my own production, based on Volkan's book and lecture, on Moreno's words and issues related to narcissism – group and individual – that have always interested me.

The fourth article, "*Fundamentals of Psychodrama: the Importance of Dramatization*" was written in 2004. In 2003, I was invited to participate in a round-table discussion addressing the theme of "Fundamentals of Psychodrama" at the IV Ibero-American Psychodrama Congress in Buenos Aires. In fact, I was already fully engrossed in reading about the neural substrate of trauma, in other words, how trauma and child abuse affect victims' brains. Le Doux (1996) and Levine (1999) were authors that I had researched for a long time. I had made drawings of brain schemes and really tried to understand why, many years after the trauma is over, clients still have symptoms.

I was interested in the fact that psychodrama is an active therapeutic technique and offers a second possibility of reaction-repair. I began to be a voracious advocate of using role play to treat traumatized people.

The round-table discussion at the congress was the excuse I needed to write about and air these ideas. To a certain extent, I "pushed the limit" to emphasize dramatization as one of the most important foundations of psychodrama, and I turned to neuroscience to reinforce my argument. I must say that I still love this article to this day.

"*Psychodrama of Addiction: The Fight Between the Addictive Personality and the True Self*" is the next article, and dates from 2005. Here, it is also worth noting that I am somewhat autobiographical. I smoked for 15 years, and it took me five years to stop smoking. In fact, I stopped three times and had two relapses: I had auricular acupuncture twice and finally stopped with the help of Nicorette, a gum that is itself addictive.

I was impressed with how easy it was to relapse – just one cigarette and the whole work of abstaining for two, three years went down the drain. Also, regarding losing weight, I faced the same difficulty: I lost 22 pounds and gained them almost immediately, turning this cycle into a perverse and endless routine.

At the same time, I started treating a very elegant girl, who was a compulsive spender. She spent money beyond her real needs, causing various relationship and financial problems for herself. I started reading and researching and became fascinated by the topic. Above all, I liked to reframe addiction as a self-medication for loneliness and a lack of meaningful human contact. Any addiction, from cigarettes to cocaine, all act as instant relief for a perennial, never-ending pain.

In 2007 I wrote the article *"Steps to Successful Dramatization"*. In addition to being a psychotherapist, I have been a psychodrama teacher and supervisor for many years, and I also direct supervisory groups. My big challenge, therefore, is to help my students use dramatization as a working and research tool in psychodynamics of clients.

When a therapist proposes constructing and dramatizing a scene to the client, they leave their comfort zone – sitting and looking like an empathetic intellectual. They need to get up, be in evidence, walk around the room and propose an action. Young therapists fear being ridiculous, not knowing how to continue the dramatization or complete it, preferring to stick to verbal communication, just asking or explaining, proposing something for the client to think about.

In this text, I am very didactic, and I practically give a gift to all my students, showing exactly how I do it and why I do what I do. I hope this will help them!

"Psychosocial Drama of Envy: Throw the First Stone if You Dare" is the next article, completed in 2011. People who have been abused/neglected during childhood have a serious disturbance with the notion of personal worth and self-esteem (CUKIER, 1998, p. 41-66), as this accounting depends on the ability to create a secure attachment relationship at an early age. Whether overestimating or undervaluing themselves, the way a person evaluates themselves has a strong impact on how they will relate to others throughout their lives.

Envy is one of those relational possibilities and causes immense problems for human beings; a feeling that is considered not very noble, it appears in the clinic in disguise, often camouflaged by the contrary claim: "others are envious of me".

Approaching it directly is often a one-way trip, in which an offended patient abandons psychotherapy. So, what should you do then? This is the question that motivated about three years of research, reading many texts and the article you will read.

Finally, *"Post-traumatic Stress: Current Trends, Treatment and Psychodrama"* is the last article in this book. Post-traumatic stress is one of the possible consequences of child abuse and domestic violence, even though we face a situation more often associated with soldiers and war veterans.

In 2014, one of the volumes of the Psychotherapeutic Networker Magazine described the various methods of treatment for this syndrome, highlighting the most recent active approaches and not even mentioning psychodrama. Furthermore, the author posed a question about what had happened to the old psychodynamic schools, whose treatments now seemed obsolete. I was very irritated while reading that article, realizing that the psychodramatic approach, which I thought (and still do think) was so efficient, was not valued. I decided to research and write about it, as well as verifying the effectiveness of the other recent approaches that the author had mentioned.

To sum up, this collection of articles shows my journey over the last 10 years. I hope it will nourish your mind with ideas and, above all, mobilize you to consider your personal moment when embarking on some scientific research. For me, this is the key that arouses my curiosity and gives me the energy to read and study.

References

BEATTIE, Melody. **Codependent no more:** how to stop controlling others and start caring for yourself. São Paulo: Nova Era, 1998.

BRADSHAW, John. **Healing the shame that binds you.** Rio de Janeiro: Rosa dos Ventos, 1997.

CUKIER, Rosa. **Emotional survival:** Childhood Pain Relived in the Drama of Adult Life. São Paulo: Ágora, 1998.

LE DOUX, Joseph. **The emotional brain:** the mysterious underpinnings of emotional life. Rio de Janeiro: Objetiva, 1996.

LEVINE, Peter A. **Waking the tiger:** healing trauma. São Paulo: Summus, 1999.

MILLER, Alice. **The drama of the gifted child**: the search for the true self. São Paulo: Summus, 1997.

VOLKAN, Vamik. **Bloodlines:** from Ethnic Pride to Ethnic Terrorism. New York: Farrar, Strausand Giroux, 1997.

CODEPENDENCY: DO YOU KNOW ANYONE WHO SUFFERS FROM THIS EVIL?

Someone once jokingly said that the difference between human beings and animals is not so much to do with being rational, but rather to do with the fact that humans have relatives. Perhaps due to the fact of being born "semi-prepared" and having a long childhood under the care of someone who helps them survive, human beings are the animals who engage longer and more in-depth with their predecessors and successors. Father, mother, brothers and sisters, grandparents, parents-in-law, uncles, aunties and cousins... this makes us completely unique and is also the source of our biggest problems!

This is the case with codependency, a type of emotional and bonding pathology, described by human behavior experts in the USA. The first studies date back to 1983, and despite not yet being classified in the DSM-IV, various books[1] have been written on this topic, including one already translated into Portuguese[2].

Firstly, the description of this condition included only families of alcoholic patients, but over time its meaning has been expanded and currently the term codependency also refers to the conduct of families and relatives of people who have some sort of serious and chronic, physical or emotional problem.

"A codependent person is someone who lets the behavior of another person control his/hers and who is, in turn, obsessed with controlling the behavior of the other person."

Everything begins with the fact of finding ourselves connected (because of love, obligation or duty) to someone who is very complicated, physically or emotionally ill, and due to this illness, self-destroys or gives up on living, and apparently needs our support and constant care. This person could be a child who was born with a handicap, an adult suffering from depression, a wife or lover who has anorexia, a brother who did not

---

[1] See Cormac (1986).
[2] Cf. Beattie (1994).

do well in life, a sister who is always getting into trouble and seems to be too fragile to resolve her problems, an alcoholic father.

To sum up, the important thing is not who this person is or what illness they have; the core of the issue is in ourselves, in how we let this person affect our behavior and the ways in which we try to influence their behavior or "help them". It is, first and foremost, a reaction to the other´s self-destruction, which ends up destroying us. We become victims of other people's illnesses, and the more we make an effort to make this person give up their addiction or change their attitude towards life, the less they get better and the more devastated we become. It seems like our life revolves around them, we do not act on our own will, but rather we react to how the patient is: if they are well, we are well, we make plans, we are hopeful; when they turn to drinking or get depressed, we put off going to the cinema, we abandon the projects and we feel terrible.

Many therapists probably live through this or attend people who have experienced similar situations. Perhaps, what many may not be aware of, is that some scientists consider this behavior of chronic help to the other in itself an emotional, serious and progressive disorder. They even say that the codependent wants and seeks complicated people to connect with and can only be happy this way.

It does not seem to me to be this way, as many codependents that I have attended were people who were tired of suffering and who sincerely wanted to change; but whether due to upbringing, religion or personal guilt, they were not able to disconnect.

Some common characteristics of codependents have caught my attention: they are usually people who have a generous nature, they come from emotionally disturbed families and ever since their childhood have wanted to fix things they believed to be wrong. They tend to make themselves responsible and guilty for everything, they are immensely dependent on love, praise, and other people's validation, and they think they can handle certain situations better than others. They lie to themselves saying that "things will get better tomorrow"; "this is the last time", and they doubt whether they will be happy in the future or if they will ever find true love.

Codependents find it difficult being around people, having fun and being spontaneous. They alternate over-affectionate care for the person who is ill with aggressive and rude ways of dealing with them; as the years pass by they increasingly feel unhappier, depressed, isolated and violent. Not rarely, they have eating disorders (either eating too much or not enough) and they end up having some kind of addiction (cigarettes, alcohol, sedatives, etc.).

Generically, this illness is associated to various forms of child abuse, and codependents basically have difficulties in five areas:

1. Low self-esteem.

    1. Difficulties in setting boundaries.
    2. Difficulties in recognizing and assuming their own reality.
    3. Difficulties in taking care of their needs as an adult.
    4. Difficulties in expressing their emotions moderately.
    5. Is there any cure for codependency? There is no simple answer to this question. In the USA, self-help groups have been set up - such as alcoholics anonymous groups for family members - where they try to discuss and offer support to codependents.

My own experience has shown that psychotherapy, especially psychodrama, which is an approach that favors the study of bonding, is often very useful in cases where the codependent is disillusioned with their own potential to change the other person's life and begins to really want to change their own life. Treatment helps and encourages the patient to undertake the necessary changes, to face their abusive past and to change their attitude concerning their ill relative so that they can regain a healthier way of living, even if the relative still wants to die.

References

BEATTIE, Melody. **Codependent no more:** how to stop controlling others and start caring for yourself. São Paulo: Nova Era, 1998.

CERMAK, T. L. Diagnostic criteria for codependency. **Journal of psychoactive drugs,** n.18, v.1, p. 15-20, 1986.

CUKIER, Rosa. **Emotional survival:** Childhood Pain Relived in the Drama of Adult Life. São Paulo: Ágora, 1998.

MELLODY, Pia. **Facing Codependence.** San Francisco: Harper & Row Publishers, 1989.

THE PSYCHODRAMA OF MANKIND.
IS IT REALLY UTOPIAN?

"A truly therapeutic procedure cannot have less an objective than the whole of mankind" (MORENO, 1992, p. 119).

"I predict sociometry and psychodrama will have an important place in the history of sociology as it will be written in the year 2000" (ibidem, p. 87).

"We assumed, naively perhaps, that if a war can spread to encircle the globe, it should be equally possible to prepare and propagate a worldly sociometry. But this vision did not come out of nowhere. Once an entire community was successfully treated by sociometric methods, it seemed to us, at least theoretically, possible to treat an infinitely large number of such communities by the same methods — in fact, all the communities of which human society consists" (ibidem, p. 228).

"The sociometric experiment will end in becoming total, not only in expansion and extension, but also in intensity, thus marking the beginning of a political sociometry" (ibidem, p. 228-9).

Moreno's pretension to treat the whole of humanity by psychodrama has always seemed exaggerated and improbable to me, utopian dreams of a man who, besides aspiring to bigger importance and recognition than he had in life, also made predictions for the distant year 2000, which he would never witness.

Having said that, I have just returned from the 13th International Congress on Group Psychotherapies held in London. It is August 1998, very near the year 2000. I came back thinking differently, I wanted to review these words of Moreno's, so I read them carefully. I heard things at this congress that repeatedly reminded me of Moreno. I am writing this paper so I can share my recent findings with you.

11

I was particularly impressed by the core theme of the keynotes, the plenaries that began the works at the congress every day. The presenters, worldwide renown professionals in scientific production, belonged to an inter-area of interest intertwining history, sociology, anthropology, politics, and psychology. Their main concern was to be able to understand and contain the escalation of the so-called political and ethnic wars.

The Stockholm International Peace Research Institute estimates the number of Major Armed Conflicts[3] to have reached a plateau since 1986 – around 30 conflicts in 25 localities –, although they have grown in intensity and dangerousness. What alarmingly increased, however, was the number of Minor Conflicts, more known as Ethnic Terrorism[4].

The word ethnicity comes from the Greek word *ethnos,* meaning company, people or tribe. After World War II, as a United Nations (UN) initiative, the term "ethnic group" was adopted as a substitute for the term "race", due to the connotations of biological inferiority or superiority which the Nazis gave to this word.

In spite of that, new words do not exorcize old problems. National civility, which used to allow people from different cultures in the same nation[5] to live together in peace, has been defeated by ethnic hatred, and millions of people have died since then in those "confrontations among neighbors'".

In Yugoslavia, for instance, it is estimated that 65,000 people died on account of ethnic conflicts; in Bosnia-Herzegovina, 55,000[6]; in Croatia, around 10,000; and in Rwanda, deaths are reaching one million already. And how many more people may be dying in conflicts in Afghanistan, Algeria, Angola, Azerbaijan, Bangladesh, Burundi, Cambodia, Colombia, Georgia, Guatemala, India, Indonesia, Iran, Iraq, Israel, Liberia, Myanmar,

---

[3] Major Armed Conflict is defined as a prolonged conflict between military forces from two or more governments and which generates over 1,000 deaths.

[4] Terrorist attacks inspired by ethnic and/or religious differences, directed by individuals or small groups.

[5] The difference between nation and ethnic group resides in the fact that nation implies an autonomous politics and the establishment of frontiers, or at least organizations which will create roles, ranking and status. Most nations are made of more than one ethnic group and some scientists refer to ethnic groups as subnations.

[6] Research conducted by Tibeau and Bijak in 2004, identified 102,000 deaths and estimated the following division: 55,261 were civilians and 47,360 were soldiers. From the civilians: 16,700 were Serbians, while 38,000 were Bosnian and Croatian. From the soldiers: 14,000 were Serbians, 6,000 were Croatian and 28,000 were Bosnian. (Nilsen, Av Kjell Arild; Norwegian News Agency)

Peru, the Philippines, Somalia, Sri-Lanka, Sudan, Turkey, England, and Zaire?

Our attention is turned to the barbarism of these conflicts where human rights are completely ignored; genocide is a frequent goal and not even the ethic codes of traditional wars are adopted. We no longer talk about the "extermination of a population"; nowadays "ethnic cleansing" is the word of command, and it aims at not leaving alive any person who belongs to another ethnic group or who remembers the lands and houses they owned. Décio de Freitas (1998) shows us that many of those who fight and kill one another may be ethnically similar in history, in blood, in language, and even in religion. Intolerance focuses not on macroscopic differences, but on subtle alliances; there is loyalty to a small ethnic group and not to the greater nation. Revenge is claimed for past offenses; we seek, transgenerationally and at any cost, to restore the dignity of the people themselves.

You must be wondering: What does Moreno have to do with that? Well, the old dream of treating the whole of mankind is current in Europe - at least that is what I extracted from the books of some of those renowned lecturers.

The Turkish psychiatrist, Vamik Volkan (1997), for example, affirms that from all these conflicts originated an increased demand for a change concerning the concept of diplomatic work, as it now also includes the psychological dimension of events and not just its economics and social character.

Most ethnic conflicts involve complex matters related to the *identity of the large groups* involved and cannot be negotiated by political diplomacy alone. Nor does traditional international diplomacy work in these issues, as it is not a question of two distinct peoples fighting, but of the internal struggles of the same people. Donald Horowitz (Volkan, 1997), a political scientist, defends the idea that the amount of passion expressed in ethnic conflicts demands an explanation that takes into consideration emotions.

The identity of large groups

Human beings have always lived in emotionally linked groups, such as clans or tribes. "Ethnic group" is the contemporary term for this phenomenon, defining a number of people who all have in common: their place of origin, ancestors, traditions, religious beliefs, and language.

Besides these characteristics, people from the same ethnic background also share a myth of inauguration, a kind of grandiose history about the origin of their group, that includes a concept of generational biogenetic continuity and lends the group some special and unique characteristics, making it different from all the others.

The perception of one's own tribe or group as being human and superior to the others - consequently seen as subhuman - is a universal phenomenon that intrigues anthropologists. The ancient Chinese, for example, called themselves people, and other races *Kueri*, hunting spirits. The American Apaches called themselves *indeh* (persons) and others *indah* (enemies). In English, the term "barbarian" refers to a foreigner.

Initially, neighboring tribes used to compete for survival items such as food and water. Over time, as their survival was assured, other items became the target of competition; superfluous ones, such as skins and material goods, but which increase the self-esteem of those who possess them and become representations of power. These symbols, in turn, gain colors, flags, songs and other indicators of the shared identity and the mythical story of the group.

Ethnicity[7] is an aspect of personal identity; it is a social, non-biological identity, and it goes beyond genetic considerations. Its major peculiarity is that it is felt only when one group interacts with another, as if it were a potential possibility that only manifests itself through interacting with the different. A certain degree of ethnocentrism is common and healthy in all groups, but it may dangerously escalate into into a type of racism.

Personality and psychodynamics of ethnic groups

Very little is known so far about how large groups function
(FREUD, 1920).

Freud made some attempts to study group phenomena. Before him, other authors, namely the French sociologist, Gustave Le Bon (FREUD, 1920), and the British author, McDougall (FREUD, 1920) had also tried to shed some light on the matter. They found that whenever an individual takes part in a group, they lose their habitual identity and

---

[7] In Yugoslavia, for example, it is people from the same blood, but different religions, that kill one another.

experience an increase in emotionality and suggestibility, as well as a decrease in intellectual and cognitive abilities. Freud attributed these phenomena to the libido, which he credited with creating and maintaining love ties in a group. According to him, the group mind was structured in a manner similar to that of family models; love among group members and their ability to influence one another would be proportional to the love and respect achieved by the leader of the family. As to hostilities among members, those were attributed to poorly resolved oedipal questions.

Volkan believes that this explanation is incomplete and does not clarify the issue of aggressiveness in human relationships, because a strong sense of group identity sometimes leads to brutal acts of violence. According to Volkan, Freud himself was cautious in applying his findings in individual psychology to group psychology. In 1932, in a letter[8] entitled "Why war?", Albert Einstein asked Freud whether there was any way whatsoever of preventing wars from happening. Freud was pessimistic in saying that there was no way to eliminate the aggressive inclination of human beings. Many other psychoanalysts have made contributions to large group psychology, without, however, arriving at more comprehensive or satisfactory explanations than Freud's.

Fortunately, new efforts have been made. In 1978, the then Egyptian president, Anwar Al Sadat, made an indirect invitation to mental health professionals to work together with diplomats, in an effort to understand and undo the psychological barrier, which, in his words, constituted 70% of the problem between Arab Israelis. A grant was obtained from the United Nations Fund and a small committee was created, within the American Psychiatry Association, which held meetings in various places in Europe. From 1980 to 1986, Egyptian, Palestinian, Israeli, and American psychiatrists and diplomats split and joined small discussion groups as a way to facilitate the dialog between the parties of the dispute. This effort brought new and valuable insights into both the behavior and the identity of emotionally linked large groups.

Culturally unresolved mourning and transgenerational transmission

---

[8] https://en.unesco.org/courier/may-1985/why-war-letter-albert-einstein-sigmund-freud

Losses experienced by a culture as a whole, such as the killing of beloved leaders; natural disasters resulting in a high number of deaths; domination, imprisonment and humiliation of an ethnic group by another, etc., also require a process of mourning and elaboration, and an unsuccessful attempt to achieve this may cause them to become perennial.

A culture conveys its message of grief in peculiar ways. For instance, it may use mass communication to report an event or create anecdotes as a way of elaborating a tragedy; execute cultural rituals to celebrate the anniversary of these traumatic events; build resistant monuments out of metal or stone to symbolize the strength with which these events will never be forgotten. Whenever a whole generation is decimated, subjugated and forbidden to cry and ritualize its loss - as in the case of the Holocaust, that marked World War II or of the Navajos, who were expelled from their land by American colonizers in 1864 -, those who survived such a tragedy are entrusted with transmitting their sentiments to their descendants, as if future generations could be entrusted with the task of mourning and elaborating once impractical to their ancestors.

To a certain degree, nothing is ever forgotten by a culture. One could analogically speak of a collective unconscious according to Jung[9], or of a co-unconscious[10], recalling Moreno, or even of post-traumatic stress disorder[11] - in short, there are group mechanisms used for gathering up and transgenerational transmitting, in a way yet unknown to science,

---

[9]Jung's collective unconscious is a broader concept than Freud's concept of the subject. Jung's concept includes, besides the repressed childhood experience, the experience phylogenetically accumulated by mankind, which functions independently from the Ego because it originates in a structure inherent to the brain. Its manifestations are found in culture in the fashioning of universal motives, which possess their own degree of attraction (SAMUELS, 1988, p. 1404-5).

[10]Moreno (1975, p. 31) describes the co-unconscious as a state shared simultaneously by all participants of the same living experience and which, therefore, can only be reproduced and represented by a group.

[11]Post-traumatic stress disorder consists of a debilitating reaction following some traumatic event. Very frequently encountered in war veterans, it also includes reactions to serious accidents, natural disasters, and violent assaults such as rape and torture. This condition causes a person to have recurring memories of the most shocking facts, which intrusively devastate their thoughts in the form of nightmares or of daytime fantasies. Sleep disorders, depression, irritability, the lack of a sense of belonging, and loneliness are also experienced.

the resentment, traumas and injustices experienced by a given generation.

Anne Ancelin Schützenberger (1997) presents numerous clinical samples of what she calls the "anniversary syndrome", where within the same family, a given tragic event - for instance, a fatal accident - is repeated in various generations, always on the same date. Another interesting report of hers is about "family secrets", which return encrypted in a given patient elected in a future generation, who, through his/her symptoms, speaks of what was once before unspeakable and unthinkable.

From the same author comes the concept of "parentification", a process of inversion of dependencies, in which children take care of their parents, guided by an implicit and complex system of merits and debts accounting, in which all that was once received by a child in the form of care, kindness and companionship must eventually be repaid to the parents. The injustices suffered by the family are also part of this accounting, and each member bears the burden of, in their own way, revenge, forgetting and demanding these injustices. There is no way to escape these family obligations without carrying with it a feeling of "amorphous and indefinable existential guilt.

It is interesting to note that, although the word "loyalty" derives from the Latin word *legalitas* (which refers to law), its real meaning is connected to an invisible interweaving of family expectations, not always manifested through justice or legality. Individuals who do not learn the meaning of justice within family relationships will tend to develop a distorted idea of social justice.

Group narcissism, resentment, revenge and fury

Would it be possible for us to consider the existence of a narcissistic group system in which the conscience of individual worth is connected to the worth of the group to which the individual belongs and, as a consequence, any attack to this group's self-esteem would trigger responses of fury and revenge aimed at restoring the group's lost dignity? We know that this is true on an individual basis. I myself (CUKIER, 1998) have previously affirmed that "children abused in their childhood are like future time bombs", as they will seek retaliation for this abuse when they have the power to do so.

In large groups, it seems to take the parallel occurrence of many factors to culminate in a reaction of revengeful fury. The presence of a fanatic leader, for example, with a childhood history of abuse and negligence, is one of these factors. Alice Miller (1993) demonstrates that, behind all great catastrophes of mankind, there were always narcissistic, sadistic leaders hurt by negligent and abusive parents who were never able to deal with the basic needs of their children. This was true for Adolf Hitler, Stalin and Nicolae Ceaușescu (a Romanian Dictator) who were cowardly spanked and humiliated in their childhood. Another predisposing variable is the present occurrence, or a still-remembered past occurrence, of an attack to "the group's pride". According to Kohut (1988), group cohesion is achieved through shared greatness, and groups will present regressive, narcissistic transformations every time this greatness is attacked. These regressive transformations of group narcissism result in narcissistic aggression, anger, fury, and revenge.

There are also culturally rooted factors favoring aggressive reactions, such as symptoms of self-repudiation or shame. This is true for Japanese people who reject the facial characteristics of their own race and undergo plastic surgeries to acquire the characteristics of majority groups, which are economically and culturally dominant.

Hugo Bleichmar (1987) calls these identifying objects or traces which we wish to possess so that their intrinsic worth may be conferred upon us (such as cars, jewelry, a certain type of eyes, etc.) "narcissistic possessions". Bleichmar also shows us how culture offers many different ways of naming reality, which carry identifying beliefs and attributes that give value to someone as an individual. That is true with possessive adjectives used in the context of genetic family inheritance. The words "my, thy, and our" literally build a bridge between objects and their possessors. Bleichmar affirms:

The word "**my**" comes across to a child as having the same meaning as when used by his/her parents in "**my child**": the parents' narcissism requires that the **child-phallus** be regarded as a product of their own. Therefore, "**my child**" stands for the child who, having been **created by me, is my own,** and therefore speaks of **myself** (ibidem, emphasis added).

Moreover, there are logical rules in the individual unconscious; for instance, the logic of social class inclusion, which assimilates the identity and value of all the elements in this class. Then it is understood why, despite impetuous fights within the same family, if someone from outside the family criticizes one of its members, because this member is considered a narcissistic property of the ego, all the other members will immediately come to his defense.

According to Anne Ancelin Schützenberger (1997), group resentment is a phenomenon connected to the injustice suffered by that particular group or by one of its members. Loyalty as a component in moral obligation makes all individuals in a group feel they have an obligation to seek equity and justice, and guilt is the punishment to whoever fails to fulfill this obligation.

"An eye for an eye, a tooth for a tooth" — that is the talionic justice[12] , which sets the rules for the final settlement of debts for our long-suffering mankind. In the end, we may all end up toothless and blind. Would Moreno be able to help us?

Moreno's suggestions for treating mankind

Moreno created the sociodrama for treating groups and collective problems, and his book "Who shall survive?" is dedicated to formulating and testing ways to make this project feasible. He defines sociodrama as "a deep action method that investigates and treats inter-group relations and collective ideologies" (MORENO, 1975, p. 411; MORENO, 1992, p. 80).

Moreno made many attempts at theorizing group behavior. He proposed a distinction between the identity process and the identification process, in his words: "Identity should be considered apart from the process of identification. It develops prior to the latter in the infant and it operates in all inter-group relations of adult society" (MORENO, 1975, p. 442). Moreno also suggested the term "identity of role" for naming what we would contemporarily call ethnic identity: "Black people consider themselves a single collective, *the Black People*, a condition which submerges all individual differences. (...) We shall call this identity, the identity of role" (*ibidem*, p. 442).

Moreno spoke many times of the differences between catharsis in sociodrama and catharsis in psychodrama, emphasizing that in sociodrama one seeks to treat questions related to identity:

---

[12] The Law of Talion [lex talionis], which belongs to the Code of Laws of Hammurabi, King of Babylon in 2500 BC, by which a penalty inflicted should correspond in degree and kind to the offense of the wrongdoer.

The protagonist on the stage is not portraying a dramatis personae, the creative output of the mind of an individual playwright, but a collective experience. He is an auxiliary ego, an emotional extension of many egos. Therefore, in a sociodramatic sense, it is not the identification of the spectator with the actor on the stage, presuming some differences between him and the character which the latter portrays. It is identity. (ibidem, p. 424).

Moreno did not address group narcissism, but came close when he affirmed that envy could be a resentment engine acting between groups:

The Jewish population in Germany may have produced more individual leaders than their numeric proportion would allow (...). As the majority of the group were Germans, we can imagine the feelings of resentment which arose among the German leader groups, together with the conviction that they had more of a "natural right" than the Jewish leaders to direct the German masses of workers and farmers (MORENO, 1992, v.3, p. 130).

Besides this, the sociometric test itself, through its calculation of choices, rejections, and neutralities, ends up addressing the narcissistic question at its core, provoking reactions often catastrophic and which Moreno pointed out and attempted to explain. On sociometric procedures, he affirms:

[...] These procedures should be greeted favorably as they aid in bringing to recognition and into realization the basic structure of a group. But such is not always the case. They are met with resistance and even hostility by some people [...] (MORENO, 1992, v.2, p. 202).

Moreno has always been concerned about racial conflicts, and even formulated the idea of a racial quotient: "from the social interaction of the members and from their emotional expansiveness, it results in a group expression, reaching its saturation point for a certain contrasting racial element, its racial quotient" (ibidem, p.260).

In "The Black-white problem: a Psychodramatic Protocol" (MORENO, 1975, p. 425-52), he audaciously discusses the situation of

African-Americans in the United States and makes theoretical and important considerations about the process of racial discrimination and the counter-responses it generates. Moreno also elaborated the concept of a *point of racial saturation* (MORENO, 1992, v.3, p. 216), in which he expresses the idea that there is a certain point beyond which a majority population becomes saturated with a minority population, which thereby favors racial discrimination.

Actually, since writing "The Words of the Father", he seems to have the firm intention of, instead of pulling out eyes and teeth, as proposed in the Talion law, only exchanging eyes and symbolically exchanging places with and understanding the existential place of "the other, the enemy, the different". That is what he does in his "Nazi Prayer", showing himself as capable of exchanging roles, even with the enemies of the Jewish people, to which he belonged:

> *Oh God,*
> *Our race is like healthy green grass,*
> *Other races are like weeds that suffocate the*
> *grass*
> *And for it to end*
> *Uproot the weeds and destroy them!*
> *(MORENO, 1992, p. 240)*

His conceptualization of *axiodrama* - a sociodrama focused on matters of ethics and value - also denotes a concern with the community context in that it proposes discussing and dramatizing the so-called "eternal truths", such as justice, beauty, truth, perfection, eternity, peace, etc.

Moreno was very deeply connected to his time, though also deeply critical of the achievements of this time. He used to disqualify our over robotized age, full of technical devices which lack life and spontaneity and substitute human relationships. However, he did not hesitate to use this same technology in spreading his sociocratic methods; he made use of the cinema and suggested, in a chapter written in co-authorship with John K. Fischel at the end of his book *Psychodrama*, possible ways of adapting spontaneity methods to television resources.

It is advisable organizing psychodramatic sessions to be transmitted to the world from a TV station. [...] It is advisable to organize live and dramatized newscasts that can be transmitted to the world through TV stations. This is healthier than the usual photographic newscast of events; it is a tool through which the alive and creative genius may, on this planet, communicate directly and instantaneously with its peers" (MORENO, 1975, p. 482-3).

Moreno was against dolls, mechanical toys, aseptic baby bottles, in short, against technology. I, however, keep thinking that, were he still among us, he would undoubtedly find a way to use the Internet as a forum for discussions, a free tribune, and, why not perhaps role-playing via satellite, making it possible for archenemies to exchange roles, or find that fear, pain, horror, loneliness, humiliation, pride, all of these are attributes, shared by all the human species and not only by a particular tribe.

Conclusion

I would like to finish this article by paying tribute to those, among us Brazilians, who have put their best efforts in pursuing Moreno's sociocratic lead. I am talking about the growth and creativity of various groups and schools of Spontaneous Theater, groups doing socio dramatization work with rural communities, needy populations and minorities discriminated against on account of health problems and poverty, and also community services dealing with domestic violence. I am also enchanted with the possibility of using the theater as a means for working with large groups. To summarize, I believe that we, Brazilians, have some of that Morenian audacity, necessary to push this social project forward.

I mentioned audacity because a job like this does indeed require a great deal of courage. Volkan (1997), - with his group of diplomats, politicians, historians and psychoanalysts - held only a few and small verbal meetings, all closed, with a restricted audience. Even so, reading his book gives us a measure of how tense and dangerous the environment in these meetings can be.

Imagine if ethnic confrontations could happen on TV, all conducted by a skilled psychodramatist, and if millions of people could interact, sending in questions, contributing arguments, facts. I am amazed by the thought of it!

However, how many of us would have the audacity to conduct such psycho-political sociodramas? Directing sociodramas and large audiences is a task for few. In fact, no psychodrama school prepares us enough for that. Moreno gives us ideas, but we have a lot to learn. I have witnessed chaotic sociodrama sessions with directors who were lost and ashamed, and I have even watched shoes being thrown by an enraged audience. Large groups, such as those described by Freud, seem to function like a wild animal to be tamed, and words, as used in individual communication do not convey their messages in the same way (maybe applause or cheers would do the trick, and maybe we should seek the help of mass communication professionals).

I do not know exactly how to go about it, but I have a feeling that we must learn in a group how to deal with groups. The experience of studying Moreno, such a complex writer and author, with GEM[13], in a group, bit by bit, patiently and persistently, has taught me that everything is possible whenever a large number of people really wish for it.

Volkan (1997) suggests, at the end of his book, that maybe it is necessary to articulate great intercultural, intergenerational, and multigenerational apologies. Not long ago we watched Mikhail Gorbachev apologize on behalf of Russia for the massacres in Poland; the Catholic Church has also apologized for its apathy toward the extermination of Jews during World War II.

In conclusion, I wish Moreno could accept my apologies for the many times I regarded him as a foolish dreamer, alone up on a hill, looking at a future only he could glimpse at. Maybe he was indeed a fool, but he is not the only one. There are many fools like him trying to help the United Nations so we can at least have A FUTURE.

REFERENCES

BLEICHMAR, H. (1987). **O narcisismo.** Estudo e Enunciação da Gramática Inconsciente Editora Artes Médicas, Porto Alegre, Brasil.

BOSZMORMENYI-NAGY, I. (1983). **Invisible Loyalties:** reciprocity in intergenerational family therapy; Amorrortu Editores, Buenos Aires.
CUKIER, R. (1998)-**Emotional survival:** childhood pain relived in the drama of adult life. Ágora, São Paulo.

---

13 GEM - Daimon: Study Group of Moreno's Works at the Daimon Clinic, in São Paulo.

FREITAS, D. (1998) "**Masks of the neo racismo**", Jornal O Globo, August 9, Porto Alegre,Brazil.

FREUD, Sigmund (1921). **Group psychology and the analysis of the ego.** *In*: _______Complete work, Amorrortu Editores, v.18, p. 63-136, Buenos Aires, Argentina.

KOHUT, H. (1980). **Self-Psychology and the Humanities**: **Reflections on a New Psychoanalytic Approach**, W. W. Norton & Company, New York, USA.

MILLER, Alice. **Breaking down the wall of silence.** New York: Meridian Book, 1993.

MORENO, Jacob Levy (1975) **Psicodrama,** Cultrix, São Paulo.

_______. **The words of the father.** New York: Beacon House, 1977.

_______. **Who shall survive? Foundations of sociometry, group psychotherapy and sociodrama**. New York: Forgotten Books, 2018.London.

.

SAMUELS, A. (1998). **The father:** contemporary Jungian perspectives. New York: New York University Press.

SCHUTZEMBERGER, Anne A. 1995- **Querer sarar: o caminho da cura.**: Vozes, Rio de Janeiro

VOLKAN, Vamik. **Bloodlines:** from Ethnic Pride to Ethnic Terrorism. New York: Farrar, Strausand Giroux, 1997.

PSYCHOTHERAPIST FATIGUE: SECONDARY POST-TRAUMATIC STRESS DISORDER[14]

Very often, my friends and acquaintances, laics in psychotherapy, ask me if I take my patients' problems home with me. Somehow, they seem to believe that we, psychotherapists, leave our offices in a worried state, carrying the weight of other peoples' problems and can hardly sleep at night.

I have always calmly answered that that is not exactly so as therapists are required to take rigorous professional training, which enables them to distinguish their own contents from those of their patients.

That may be a good answer for lay people – that will remain so, and also deeply amazed at our absolute skill –, although a very unsatisfactory one if we really wish to reach the deep nature of this subject. Even Freud (1910, p. 1565), who defined the countertransference phenomenon as "an emotional response from the therapist facing his/her client", was somewhat superficial in this analysis.

More recently, however, due to studies conducted on professional stress and violence and its traumatic sequelae, an increasing number of authors have described a kind of biopsychosocial disease that affects those who take care of traumatized people. This "disease" has many names in the literature (FIGLEY, 1995, p. 9): "secondary post-traumatic stress disorder", "secondary victimization", "co-victimization", "vicarious traumatization"; "emotional contagion", "generational effects of trauma"; "savior syndrome"; "compassion fatigue"; "burnout therapist syndrome", among others.

These authors' studies do not focus on the patient or on how he/she may be harmed by the therapist; on the contrary, they focus on how the psychotherapist profession may be unhealthy and have a personal cost to the therapist him/herself.

There are some similarities among the different symptoms of professional stress, mainly when stress is related to excess work and bad working conditions. However, there are specific characteristics of unhealthiness occurring in the helping professions, which is the focus of

---

14 Article first published in the Psychodrama Brazilian Journal, v.10, n.1, p. 55-67, 2002.

this article. Being in contact with another's trauma and trying to help traumatized people somehow causes deep stress to the helper and, ironically, the more sensitive and devoted the helper is, the more vulnerable he/she will be to the mirror-effect of another's pain.

In this sense, I chose the term *secondary post-traumatic stress disorder*, as in my opinion it best describes what occurs in the various psychotherapy areas, and *psychotherapist fatigue* as the common term that best adapts to the language.

What is secondary post-traumatic stress disorder?

In 1980, the Diagnostic and Statistical Manual - DSM III of the American Psychiatric Association (1989, p. 264-7) included, for the first time, the diagnosis of Post-traumatic Stress Disorder (PTSD), to describe symptoms affecting people who go through a psychologically painful experience. Included in this category are unusual events of human experience that represent serious threats to one's own life or one's children and close relatives' lives, such as natural disasters (earthquakes, accidents) or intentional disasters (torture, power abuse). This manual also clarifies that the trauma may be directly or indirectly experienced, through learning about threats and damage to the physical integrity of friends, relatives or close people.

Thus, SPTSD - Secondary Post-traumatic stress disorder - may be defined as natural behaviors and emotions that arise from knowing about traumatic events experienced by a significant other. It consists of a process of gradual emotional exhaustion, related to excessive work, but which won't be solved by going on vacation. It is a gradual erosion of the therapist's spirit and involves a loss of confidence and faith in their own capacity to help. Ayala Pines (1993, p.386-402) believes that only professionals with high ideals and motivations experience this syndrome, as if it were a strain between the professional's need to help and the real problems involved in dealing with people.

Reviewing the empirical research about this syndrome, Kahill (1988) identifies five categories of symptoms:

1. Physical Symptoms: physical exhaustion and fatigue, sleep difficulties, somatic problems like headaches, gastrointestinal disorders, influenza, etc.

2. Emotional Symptoms: irritability, anxiety, depression, guilt, feeling of helplessness.
3. Behavioral symptoms: aggressive behavior, coldness, pessimism, cynicism, drug abuse.
4. Professional symptoms: quitting the job, poor work performance, missing work, being late, excessive work without breaks, etc.
5. Interpersonal Symptoms: inability to concentrate, avoidance of contact with clients and colleagues, difficulties in personal life, etc.

Duton and Rubinstein (1995, p. 85) think that the indicators of this status reproduce in the therapist some of the symptoms of the post-traumatic stress syndrome (PTSD):

1. Stress emotions, including: sadness, mourning, depression, anxiety, fear and horror, rage, hatred, shame; 2. Intrusive images of the client's traumatic material in nightmares, for example, or in awake fantasies with visual flashes.
2. Difficulty in dealing with the client's dissociation.
3. Somatic complaints such as sleep difficulties, headaches, gastrointestinal problems and palpitations.
4. Addictive and compulsive behavior, including substance abuse, eating disorders and compulsive working.
5. Difficulties in daily social activities and private life roles, such as canceling appointments, decreased use of therapy and supervision, chronic tardiness, decreased self-care and self-esteem and a sense of isolation and alienation.
6. Physiological excitement.

Who is most vulnerable to PTSD?

To sum up, all professionals whose fundamental working tool is empathy and all people who are regularly in contact with traumatized people are potentially vulnerable to this contagious traumatization. The so-called "helping" professions (firemen, policemen and military, emergency and rescue teams) and all professions related to health (nursing, medicine, and especially psychology and psychiatry).

For many reasons, the last two professional categories are the most affected, from factors related to the choice of the profession to those related to particular working conditions.

Being a therapist: a choice or destiny?

Alice Miller (1997, p. 30-3) believes that choosing a helping profession, especially that of a psychotherapist, has more to do with fate than with choice itself. She refers to the fact that most therapists come from dysfunctional families where, from childhood, they were demanded to help, directly or indirectly, some less capable adult. Ingeniously trained from childhood to be at someone's disposal, these people have developed their empathic ability and sensitivity, which will be their favorite working tool in the future.

Empathy, an essential tool to access the client and to plan a strategy of action, makes professionals exchange places with the victims, but doing so they indirectly experience the same events that traumatized their clients. Moreover, the professional's unresolved trauma will be revived by the report of a similar experience by the client, especially if it consists of a childhood trauma, probably due to the higher vulnerability of the child and to the remembrance of their own childhood.

Many authors have developed studies on the characteristics of people who choose these professions. High ideals and generous hearts are some traits pointed out by Grosch and Olsen (1994, p. 9). They have concluded that psychology and psychiatry students constitute a group of optimistic and all-powerful young people, willing not only to make money, but also to change the world; and believe that, after hard training along with compassion and care, they will be able to transform the life of the people they are taking care of.

Freudenberg (1980) describes the "Type-A" personality, which comprises different traits such as high idealism and performance and low self-esteem; this kind of individual works harder and harder to feel more acceptable. They are excessively devoted professionals who tend to demand too much from themselves and very often substitute social life for work. Some psychoanalysts (ALLEN, 1979, p. 42 and p. 171-5) believe that being successful in their careers may compensate for childhood disappointments, for instance, unresolved fraternal rivalries, or that it will represent a late Oedipal victory.

In our area, Victor C. Dias (1987, p. 187-95) brings attention to the solitude of psychotherapists, who, accustomed to open and sincere communication, devoid of the usual social dissimulations and hypocrises, end up restricting their relationships to people who also communicate like that, usually meaning people who have also undertaken psychological therapy. This is the trap which leads the therapist to be more and more solitary, tending to arrogance, inadequacy and social aggressiveness.

What causes stress to professionals?

The systemic theory seeks to understand the person through the impact that the systems that involve them have on his/her life. The concept of circular causality may be applied to the therapist's fatigue issue (see figure 1). This figure indicates pressures arising from various relationship systems involving health care professionals.

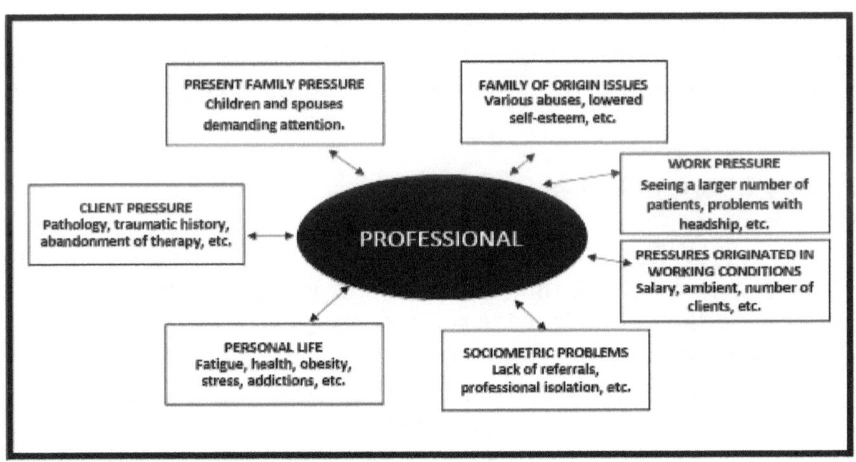

FIGURE 1 - THE MULTISYSTEM OF PRESSURE ON THE HELPING PROFESSIONAL

Present family and personal life pressure

Some authors associate career success with the professional's middle age, showing that generally a professional attains their top effectiveness between 40 and 50 years of age. It is also at this age that life events usually bring dissatisfaction (marriage crisis, aging, women's menopause, children's marriage). Experiencing these existential crises and, at the same time, taking care of people in need may be exhausting and stressful.

Moreover, Grosh and Olsen (1994) conveniently describe another frequent situation to us psychotherapists: while we spend hours and hours on end listening to and being empathetic to others, we neglect our own families and ourselves. After long hours listening to patients, how many of us really feel willing to handle our children's and companions' routine complaints, or even how many of us feel like doing physical exercises or having a balanced meal? A study conducted by Michael Mahoney[15] showed that problems such as overweight, difficulties in sleeping and generalized exhaustion, were some of the most frequent complaints among the interviewed psychotherapists.

Sensitive heroes to our clients, we suddenly transform ourselves into careless participants of our family systems and neglectful of our own bodies.

Family of origin issues

According to Bowen and his self-differentiation theory, people handle their family of origin difficulties with a large variety of ongoing responses from cutting their families off to completely merging with them. There is no self-differentiation in any of these radical solutions. Total fusion or withdrawal leaves work to be done, which will receive a response in the individual's contemporary relationships.

The professional environment is extremely propitious to becoming a second family, where people play or try to play roles similar to those of

---

15 Personal Communication in a workshop on "The personal life of the psychotherapist". Michael Mahony holds an MD and PhD from Stanford University and is author of various books on the Cognitive and Constructivism approach.

their families of origin and where they expect to put an end to the former emotional drama, although they just keep repeating it.

Client pressure

In this item, in addition to the constant concern with the evolution and severity of the cases of which we take care, I would like to point out another professional fatigue factor. Berkowitz (1987, p. 85-9) describes the "non-reciprocal attention" phenomenon. The author explains that psychotherapists seem to be prepared to deal with others' pain and stress, but they do not seem prepared for the patient's lack of reciprocity. The act of constantly giving, in a one-way relationship with no feedback or perceivable success, is hard for anyone, especially to someone who has become a therapist to understand their own dysfunctional roots.

The therapist's work implies a constant "affective turn on and off" with the other person. Many times, at the top of a therapy process we are supposed to be successful in, the patient quits therapy or is abruptly withdrawn from therapy by paying parents, with no explanations, which makes the loss and mourning process difficult, demanded by any detachment. Young therapists, mainly, feel deeply upset at these solitary losses, at the sudden divestment of a relationship they supposed to be strong and productive.

Work pressure, sociometric problems, pressure originated in working conditions

The psychotherapy profession has some unrealistic expectations in terms of healing people in a profitable and elegant way. Unfortunately, working conditions, our consultation fees, as well as our sociometry are often unsatisfactory. Our colleagues who perform community services experience various kinds of frustration, from location and attendance to their services to the lack of remuneration. "The institution care client is one who does not pay, often does not show up and never improves", says a humorous quotation about the reasons for stress.

Even those who have a private office very often embitter the lack of paying clients, a low remuneration from healthcare insurance, the very instability of a self-employed career - consequently lacking gratification from the professional life.

Professional abuse and therapist fatigue

The therapist's stress may lead to a careless and abusive service to patients. Some colleagues compensate for their low consultation fee by seeing many patients on the same day, or organizing excessively large groups of people, in detriment of quality work and their own personal health. The therapist's unrealistic expectations may also affect the client's development. The urgency to be regarded as useful and to be reassured of their professional ability may transform the therapist's compassion into pressure on the patient to perform changes in their life.

On the other hand, a patient's relapse may lead the therapist to feeling inefficient and frustrated. Taking Kohut's ideas about the narcissistic issue as a starting point, William Groch and David Olsen (1994, p. 57) describe some psychotherapists' arrogance and "God Complex". They believe that as they did not experience enough mirroring and empathy in their first childhood years, now they can compensate for their desire to be appreciated and esteemed using the patient for this complementary role.

In this sense, the objective of helping careers is paradoxical: in one aspect they represent a way to transcend oneself; in another they may well serve as a means to gaining others' consideration.

Dealing with people who tend to idealize us leads to two kinds of common mistakes: 1. we may assume that they are dead right, that we are really special and so we keep on doing things to maintain their opinion about us; 2. we may become so anxious with this load of idealization that we will do anything to disappoint them, acting wrongly, making stupid mistakes, or being too symmetric towards the patient.

Actually, the therapist's role implies a certain power, which we must be prepared to assume - without excesses and for a while only. I always remember a supervisor who told me to be absent once in a while and not always replace sessions. The therapists' imperfections help to adjust this patients' excessive idealization.

Conclusion: prevention and treatment

Therapists can use many resources to take care of their personal health, but all of them invariably imply a change of work and life routine.

Distributing the number of patients better, having reasonable mealtime breaks and doing physical exercises are some of these resources, which as simple as they may appear, are extremely hard to put into practice.

It is not just a matter of working less; you must substitute part of the financial, professional and narcissistic acknowledgment which comes from a booked-up agenda, for the growing awareness that we are as vulnerable as our patients and that there is no possible way to support others' needs if we don't take care of our own needs.

Another desirable resource is to balance clients' attendance activities with didactic activities, such as giving classes, lectures or institutional work. That makes the therapist move around, talk to other people, get into more symmetrical relationships than those with their patients.

Therapy and supervision groups are also very important, as long as they represent a safe place where the professional can expose him/herself without fearing retaliation or personal critics. In my point of view, a good supervision group does not exceed 6 or 7 colleagues and implies an intimate work of constructing the professional's role. Large groups favor idealizations and defenses that end up destroying the genuineness of the information.

Another kind of group support that reduces professional isolation is organizing small study groups on an issue jointly selected. These "groups of equals", in addition to being productive (recycling professionals and producing written work), provide a symmetrical relationship that is less formal than the supervision. Almost naturally, colleagues share their working difficulties in the clinic and offer emotional support to delicate issues (such as a lack of clients, sessions that are seemingly ill-conducted, "therapist's love and hatred towards clients", tips about a service that has been worrying us, among others). Personally, I am strongly in favor of this resource.

Participating in congresses, experiences and research on the working area also helps the therapist to keep a healthy interest in their own personal practice.

I think it extremely important that we recognize these issues related to our professional performance and would very much appreciate it to have them discussed more often in our congresses. I believe that shame is associated with this matter, as we present to one another as semi-gods, and admitting our needs might be taken for some kind of personal fault or failure.

The Greek myth of Asklepius[16], god of healing and father of medicine, gives me support to conclude this text.

Asklepius, son of the god Apollo and the mortal Koronis, was wounded before being born. His father, in a jealousy crisis upon knowing that Koronis had betrayed him, ordered her to be burnt alive. However, when he found she was pregnant, he pulled the infant from her womb and gave it to Chiron, the Centaur, to teach him the art of healing. Chiron, in turn, half human and half god, could never be healed from a wound caused by Hercules. Thus, Chiron, the healer who needed to heal himself, taught Asklepius the art of healing, the ability to find seeds of light and to feel comfortable in the darkness of distress.

The paradox of the helping professions lies in the fact that the healer heals, but at the same time remains wounded. There isn't a human being with no wounds, and despite the excellence of our psychotherapies, they do not exclude us from our own humanity.

REFERENCES

ALLEN, Dwight W. Hidden stresses in success. **Psychiatry**, n. 42, p. 171-5, 1979.

BOWEN, Murray. **De la família al individuo**. Paidos, 1998.

BERKOWITZ, Martin. Therapist survival: maximizing generativity and minimizing burnout. **Psychotherapy in Private Practice**, v.5, n.1, p. 85-9, 1987.

DIAS, V. R.C.S. **Psychodrama:** theory and practice. São Paulo: Ágora, 1987.

FIGLEY, R C. Working with people with PTSD: research implications In: ______. **Compassion fatigue**. New York: Brunner/Mazsel Inc, 1995.

FIGLEY, R. C. **Compassion fatigue.** Nova York: Brunner/Mazsel Inc 1995.

FREUD, S. (1910). El porvenir de la terapia psicoanalitica In: Obras Completas. Madrid: Biblioteca Nueva, 1973, Buenos Aires, Argentina.

FREUDENBERGUER, Herbert. **Burnout:** the high cost of high achievement. New York: Doubleday Publisher, 1980.

GROSCH, William N..; OLSEN, David C. **When helping starts to hurt.** New York: W. W. Norton & Company, 1994.

---

16 Stanton, J.ª (1999) - Aesculapius: A modern Tale

KAHILL, Sophia. Interventions for burnout in the helping professions: a review of empirical evidence. **Canadian Journal for Counseling Review**, n. 22, v.3, p. 310-42, 1988.

ASSOCIATION, American Psychiatric (1987)- **DSM III: Diagnostic and Statistical Manual of Mental Disorders.** American Psychiatric Association Publishing.

MILLER, Alice. **The drama of the gifted child**: the search for the true self. São Paulo: Summus, 1997.

PINES, Ayala. Burnout: handbook of stress. **Psychotherapy in Private Practice 5**, v.1, p. 85-9, 1993.

STANTON, Jessica A. Aesculapius: A Modern Tale. **American Medical Association.** Available at: http://www.ama-assn.org/sci-pubs/msjama/articles/vol_281/no_5/jms90003.html. Accessed on: Apr 3, 2017.

FOUNDATIONS OF PSYCHODRAMA: THE IMPORTANCE OF DRAMATIZATION[17]

One of my colleagues from Moreno's study group (GEM) once said something very curious about round tables in congresses: no matter what the table theme is, the debaters always talk about what they like, meaning they take the opportunity to make public the points of their own interest, not necessarily the ones proposed by the organizers.

When considering the theme "Foundations of Psychodrama", two ways of approaching this soon come to mind: in the first, I would interpret the word 'foundation' as a solid basis that legitimates andauthorizes the psychodramatic practice; in the second, I would seek what seems to me to be fundamental, essential, and indispensable to Psychodrama. I confess that I was more attracted by the second possibility, as for Moreno (1999, p. 33), Psychodrama is just one of the methods of Sociatry, one of the three components of socionomy: sociodynamics, sociometry and sociatry (see Figure 1).

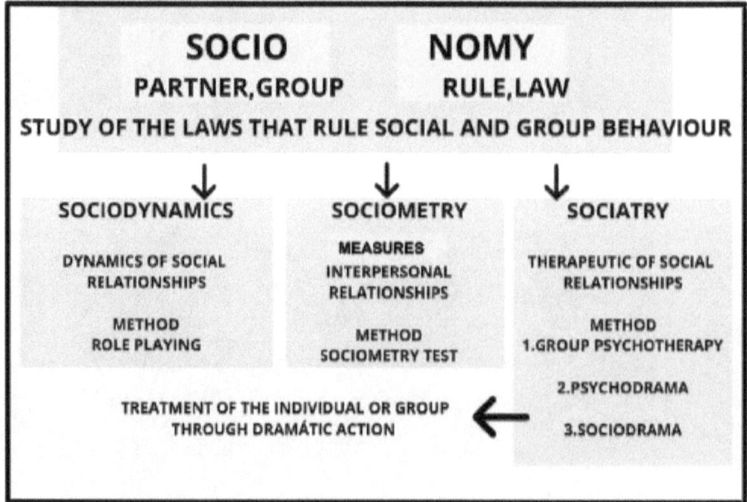

---

17 Article published in *The Brazilian Psychodrama Journal,* v.12, n.1, 2004, p.143-50. Work presented at the IV Ibero-American Congress of Psychodrama (2003).

FIGURE 1 SOCIONOMY

Searching for the foundations of Psychodrama would involve establishing the basis for the whole of socionomy, meaning describing the foundations of all of Moreno's work. I would have to mention at least the Morenian vision of the spontaneous man, his philosophy of the moment, as well as his Role Theory and Action Theory, and, honestly, I would not be able to do that in this article alone.

Therefore, I chose the second possibility, to understand the word 'foundation' as what I consider to be the basic, essential and indispensable attribute to Psychodrama.

Moreno defines Psychodrama in many ways. In one of them he says: it is the treatment of an individual or group through dramatic action (Moreno, 1992, p.183).

Personally, I consider the dramatic action one of the fundamental characteristics of Psychodrama and its absence concerns me, especially in relation to the bipersonal status. I have heard many colleagues, who are teachers and supervisors, saying that they do not like and do not dramatize in the absence of an auxiliary-ego or supplied with objects and cushions. I must reassure you that I do not doubt the efficacy of psychodrama without drama, as I know that the success of a treatment does not lie in one factor alone.

What amazes me is that some colleagues do not consider such a fantastic technical tool as dramatization, whose therapeutic value has been more and more experimentally proven. Therefore, in the next part, I would like to comment on three therapeutic aspects of the dramatic action that seem fundamental to me:

1- It provides a muscular energetic discharge, necessary for patients traumatized by various child abuses or carrying trauma sequelae of accidents (Post-traumatic Stress Disorders)

Studies on trauma and its long-lasting effects in people's lives have increasingly proved that Moreno (1959, p. 239) was right to say that "the hunger of acts" is a human physiological need just like eating, drinking and breathing.[18]

---

18 Moreno said that the *expression hunger* is, first of all, a hunger of acts, a long time before transforming into a hunger of words.

The immediate response to a stressful situation[19] releases mechanics of the sympathetic nervous system reaction, known as the "alert reaction". The animal organism gets ready for fight or flight, breathing becomes deeper, the blood flows from the stomach and intestines to the heart and to the muscles, the ongoing processes in the digestive system cease, sugar is released from the liver's reserves, the spleen twitches and releases its contents, the hypophysis stimulates the adrenal glands and the body is flooded with hormones, like adrenaline. That is an efficient preparation for activity and combat, as Walter Cannon already described in 1939 and Paul MacLean reaffirmed in 1952.

Studies developed on the animal kingdom (LEVINE, 1999) show us that when an animal is hindered from reacting, archaic brain mechanics start operating, the reptilian brain, provoking a freezing of the vital functions, thus simulating death in life. Through this trickery, pretending to be dead, the animal may succeed in being left by the predator or at least, to gain time to think of another escape strategy.

The same occurs, with some differences, to the human animal. In 1952, the American neurologist Paul MacLean described the three folded nature of the human brain, a result of our phylogenetic evolution (see figure 2).

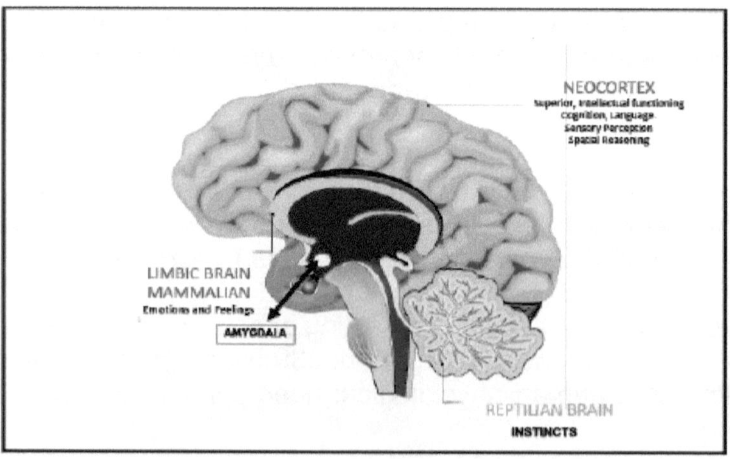

FIGURE 2 - PAUL MACLEAN, "THE VISCERAL BRAIN" (1952).

---

19 A stressful situation means any situation that leads the individual to a state of despair, whether they are fighting to preserve their lives or that of someone meaningful to them.

The brainstem is the primitive, reptilian brain. It is residual of our prehistoric past, useful for quick decisions that do not demand much thinking. The reptilian brain focuses on survival and it is driven by fear, going into action whenever we are in danger and do not have time to think. In a world where the fittest survive, the reptilian brain is concerned with getting food and not becoming food.

The central layer of the brain is the limbic part or mammalian brain, the root of emotions, humor and feelings. The neocortex is the most evolutionarily advanced part of the brain. It controls our ability to speak, think and solve problems. The neocortex affects creativity and the ability to learn and covers approximately 80% of the brain.

As we can see, the human brain is more specialized; however, as Le Doux and Van Der Kolk (1996) demonstrated, the brain is not fully functional in traumatic situations, as the neocortex undergoes functional alterations releasing hormones that make it numb (Figure 3).

The memories kept at this moment do not need to be verbalized, they are formed by sensations, visual images and motor patterns, as language is a neocortical function.

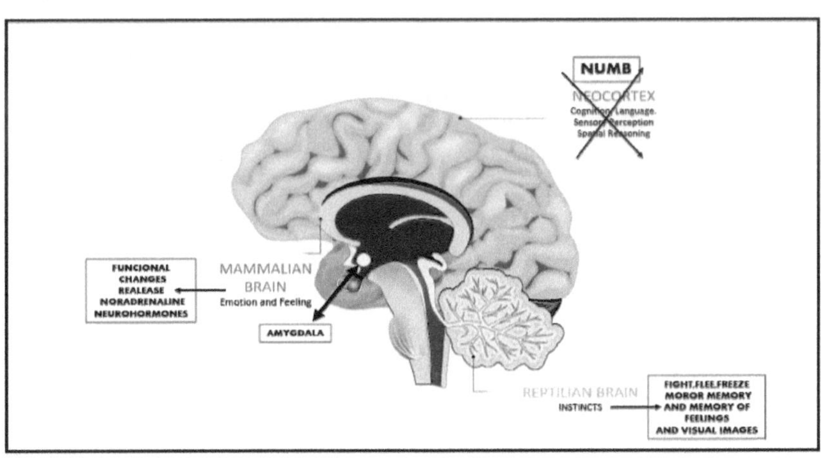

FIGURE 3 - BRAIN AND MEMORY FUNCTIONING IN

POST-TRAUMATIC STRESS

Similar to animals, human beings work with the reptilian brain when prevented from reacting. Freezing of vital functions is shown through superficial breathing and stiff muscles, simulating "rigor mortis" and an anesthetized mind, as in an ethereal state. However, contrary to the animal - which, after the danger has passed, defrosts through a noticeable body shivering - the human being intermediates these physical functions with thoughts, feelings, emotions, invisible loyalties, etc., which are results from the other two parts of the brain.

POST-TRAUMATIC STRESS

Many times, a person who was raped, for example, conceals their horror, refrains from crying, shaking and feeling ashamed to pretend to the world that nothing has happened. As a result of this non-action, their body will not recover from the trauma and the helplessness experienced at that moment.

The individual lacks an offensive action and retaking control, which are often only attained many years later, through the active repetition of the violence or abuse - this time taking the role of the abuser or of someone who holds control (many addictions are disastrous attempts to simulate control).

Dramatization allows this missing action to come about, enabling muscles to produce a safe discharge of the body's need for control recovery. I would like to remind you that psychodrama was one of the first body therapies, and Moreno already said that the body remembers what the mind forgets, especially events that take place in early childhood, even before language acquisition. The best way to recover memory from actions is through expressive methods, which address the whole person (body and mind) in the action.

2. It favors the active and responsible research of the patient in relation to their problematic

As I described above, the hindering of an offensive reaction creates a lethargic and helpless attitude before reality. Needless to say, most of our patients feel like this towards their own lives. They feel that something must be changed, but they do not feel capable of undertaking this change.

In many talk therapies - especially when interpretation is utilized - the key to the symbolic puzzle, to the meaning of feelings and thoughts, to how they relate to the past, present and future, seems to be in the therapist's hand. The patient is just the patient, they expect the therapist to do his/her job. This only reinforces their already learned fragility and helplessness.

Bustos has a small picture in his office with the saying: "what they say about me that was not disclosed by me does not fit me"; Milton Erickson (1983, p. 45) - the innovative American psychotherapist, father of modern hypnotherapy and whose methods inspired the systemic, strategic, familiar therapies, etc. – also thought that the direct interpretation of the therapist represents a rape to the unconscious of the patient, who releases a load of defenses to dissociate, deny, thus defending him/herself as much as he/she can. Into the patient's unconscious we penetrate indirectly, through the back door with much warming-up and never ahead of the patient him/herself.

Moreover, all patients have a healthy and combative portion and I particularly make my patients aware of this from day one. I always ask them what they feel like working with in that specific session and I have them play the situations they choose to work with. They are active researchers like me. Decoding their material, their emotions, decisions, it is our joint task, and often their task is more than mine.

3. It offers an element of surprise to a patient accustomed to functioning with defensive talk alone

Dramatization has no predetermined script; the psychotherapist never knows what is going to happen, much less does the client. I am often amazed at what comes up and I love to see my patients' surprised looks. I surprise them too, playing roles and counter-roles unexpectedly, seeking an interpolation of resistances very useful to stimulate spontaneous-creative answers, in other words, new answers to old situations.

Moreno (1923, p. 54) already mentioned the role of surprise in the activation of spontaneous-creative processes. In turn, Milton Erickson (1983, p. 50) used the confusion technique to induce hypnosis. For example, he would ask a person to imagine themselves getting on an airplane flying to the USA and at the end of the trip, after various commands, he would ask the person to find themselves landing in India. He knew that the surprise tactic destabilizes the intrapsychic defenses, compelling the mind to produce a different responsive energy.

The surprise element is also present in childhood traumatic situations or even in accidental traumatic situations, compelling the patient to create a defense that will give him/her back a feeling of control. The healing provided by dramatization is somehow driven by the homeopathic principle of prescribing the same factor that caused the disease, but with the objective of healing it.

I cannot think of anything more anti-morenian than a therapist verbally listening to and interpreting their patient. It would at least require triggering an internal action in the patient, in the molds of an internal psychodrama or Fonseca's relation therapy, doing reverse roles sat down or symbolically favoring their amazement and surprise, although without the benefit of muscular associations provided by body movements.

Finally, I would like to say that I believe the lack of dramatization in many psychodrama sessions is due to the unawareness of how and why to dramatize rather than to the difficulty of doing it without auxiliary egos or a group. Supervising my students, I came to the following list of most frequent questions regarding dramatization:

- How to handle issues related to therapeutic relationship: contract (timetable, location, fee, repositions); patients who do not wish to undergo dramatization, etc.
- What is the objective of dramatization? Is the objective exploratory (like a social atom), experimental (training of roles), or does it aim to repair narcissistic damage (dramatization of childhood scenes)?
- How to choose a scene to be dramatized? How to choose a scene when the patient is too talkative? Who should choose the scene, the therapist or the patient?
- How to establish time in dramatization, i.e., present, past and future? How to go from the present complaint of the patient to the past (regressive scene), or to the future (feared and desired scenes) and then come back to the here and now in the relationship with the therapist?

- How to warm up the patient and keep this warming up throughout the dramatization?
- How to decide which technique to use, among the classic ones?
- Which is best: an open scene psychodrama or an internal psychodrama?
- How not to get lost in the middle of a dramatization session?
- What to do when the session time is over in the middle of a dramatization session?
- How to finish a dramatization?

As you may conclude, my colleague - the one who said that no matter what the table theme is the debater always talks about what he/she likes - was right. I really believe dramatization to be one of the most important tools for psychodrama, and I think that better prepared students regarding these topics have less fear of using dramatization and may realize the advantages of using action techniques to help their patients.

BIBLIOGRAPHIC NOTES

CUKIER, Rosa. **"Bipersonal Psychodrama: Its Techniques, Therapists, and Clients"?** - São Paulo: Editora Ágora, 1992.
CANNON, Walter. The Wisdom of the Body, Nova York, Norton, Quoted by Anne Ancelin Schutzenberger – "Querer Sarar", Editora Vozes, Rio de Janeiro, 1995.
FONSECA, José. **Relationship psychotherapy.** São Paulo: Summus, 1999.
LE DOUX, Joseph. **The emotional brain:** the mysterious underpinnings of emotional life. Rio de Janeiro: Objetiva, 1996.
LEVINE, Peter A. **Waking the tiger:** healing trauma. São Paulo: Summus, 1999.
MORENO, Jacob Levy. **The Theater of Spontaneity.** São Paulo: Summus, 1923.
________. **Group psychotherapy and psychodrama.** Campinas: Livro Pleno, 1999.
VAN DER KOLK, B.; MCFARLANE, A. WEISAETH L. **Traumatic Stress:** the effects of overwhelming experience on mind, body and society. New York: Guilford Press, 1996.
ZEIG, K. J. **Didactic seminars on psychoanalysis by Milton H. Erickson.** Rio de Janeiro: Imago, 1983

PSYCHODRAMA OF ADDICTION: THE FIGHT BETWEEN THE ADDICTIVE PERSONALITY AND THE TRUE SELF[20]

Psycho-dramatically investigating the addictions of our clients, it is surprising to realize that the conflict born between the drug (the object of addiction) and the addicted part of the client's personality has similarities with various tragedies described in classic literature. This is the case when referring to Goethe's version of the Faust myth, for example.

In short, this is the story of the scientist, Faust, who cheats the laws of the Church in the Middle Ages to search, tirelessly and omnipotently, for the solution to the mystery of existence. He acquires knowledge of various sciences, but none of them satisfies his desire to become a kind of "God," with unlimited access to everything that occurs in nature. Aware of his human limits and not resigned to them, he is approached and seduced by Mephistopheles (the Devil), and he commits himself to delivering his soul in exchange for knowledge and intense experiencing of worldly pleasures and to have the gift of controlling time and people, causing them to sway according to his wishes. The result is disastrous. Wherever he goes, Faust spreads unhappiness. In the end, he falls victim to his own thirst for omnipotence, as he ends up hurting himself and the only woman he truly loved.

Like Faust, the addicted person tries to cheat the rules of the system. However, in this case, one is trying to circumvent not only an institution, but human nature itself, thereby challenging its essential vulnerability. We humans are powerless when faced with the lack of logic and justice in the distribution of misfortunes and differences. It is up to chance or luck attributes like the family we are born into, health, wealth, beauty, intelligence, etc. And for the future, the only certainty we have is that of our loved ones and our own deaths.

Similarly, we fear that the true self[21] of a human being will sell his soul to the addicted part in exchange for the promise of quick relief of all

---

20 Article co-written by Dinah Akerman Zimerman (Psychiatrist, with Medical Residence by the PQ Institute, FM-USP; Psychodramatist by the Sedes Sapientiae Institute), published in the *Brazilian Psychodrama Journal,* v.13, n.11, 2005, p. 85-111.
21 "True self" is used here in the sense of the personality existent before the addiction, and "addicted personality" will be the term used for the personality structured during the

the sorrows, pain, and frustrations that normal life brings about. Furthermore, the observation of several clinical cases has made it evident that the potentially addicted person seems to believe that the lives of other human beings are not the same as his/her own and do not produce the pain and disappointment that he experiences. He/she therefore feels He/she is a victim of life, requiring some extra help to finally become "normal." In fact, He/she lacks the capacity to elaborate frustrations and grief, becoming a victim, yes, but of false relief, a victim of the devil-drug that provides a state of temporary well-being and a life sentence.

Why would someone sell his /her soul to the devil or self-administer drugs that can kill, lead to imprisonment, or jeopardize their health? This is the question that motivated us to study the subject of addictions, and our conclusions will be described below.

History

Psychoactive plants have always been used by our ancestors to seek instinctive pleasures and/or pay tribute and worship gods, as in the ritual for the Baco (god) in Greece. Its prohibition began in the Middle Ages, under the influence of the Judeo-Christian doctrine, and culminated in the Enlightenment, when its consumption became a crime and the State was in charge of regulating its administration.

One of the first set of laws that regulated drug use dates from the early 20th Century and was called "Three United Nations Sisters Conventions". In the United States, the prohibition of alcohol took effect from 1919 to 1933, and it was also there where it initiated a more systematic way of treating addictions with the emergence of Alcoholics Anonymous (AA) in 1935.

This organization arose from the initiative of alcoholism sufferers working together in their efforts to resist alcohol. The symmetry of the participants (there were no doctors, competent speech makers, or health hierarchies) is the main peculiarity of this group; all participants suffer from the same problem, no one is better or worse than any other. This is merely a group of people who support each other and regard each other as equals.

---

process of becoming an addict. Purposefully, the terms *ego* and *self* were not used, so as to not enter here into the psychoanalytic and academic definitions on the theme.

During the 1960s and 1970s, the psychoactive substance usage was linked with behaviors related to rebellion and counterculture, opposing the current sociopolitical model. From 1980 there was a significant increase in the offers of synthetic elaborated psychoactive substances, which led to new repressive politics in the US, while in Europe the political view was more tolerant.

It is interesting to observe, as drug addiction researchers usually say (SILVEIRA, 2006, p. 14), that in situations where access to drugs is too easy, and even stimulated, there is a tendency towards uncontrolled consumption. However, the other extreme is equally dangerous, as repression stimulates the development of new and more dangerous ways of use, as in the case of the prohibition in the US.

Concept

Historically, addiction was thought to be a sign of moral weakness and a practice engaged in by incompetent individuals who cannot deal with reality. Today, we think of it as a physical, emotional, cognitive, and spiritual disease.

In the past, the term addiction was synonymous with drug addiction, i.e., the loss of control in the consumption of certain substances. The Diagnostic and Statistical Manual of Mental Disorders - DSM-IV-R (2002, p. 207-8) - classified drugs into 11 categories: alcohol; amphetamines or similarly acting sympathomimetics; caffeine; cannabinoids; hallucinogens; inhalants; nicotine; opioids; phencyclidine (PCP) or arylcyclohexylamines of similar action; and sedatives - hypnotics or anxiolytics. This manual also makes a distinction between disorders originated in substance use (dependence and/or abuse) and disorders induced by substances (intoxication; abstinence; delirium; dementia; psychotic conditions; amnesia and humor alterations; sexual and sleep dysfunction).

Nowadays, there is a tendency to classify addictions more flexibly including other compulsive behaviors[22], such as addiction to food,

---

22 Obsession and compulsion are related, and usually come with each other. Both refer to people consumed by something irrational. In obsession, the person has an irrational idea, and in compulsion, an irrational act. Obsession and compulsion are like post-hypnotic suggestions: they have an irresistible urgency. Some authors argue that compulsive behaviors are actions used to keep the person busy and therefore not

gambling, sex, shopping, work, shoplifting, etc. - which also induce mood swings, social isolation, shame and despair. New terms are rising, such as "Compulsive Spectrum Disorder", or "Affective Spectrum Disorder", or even "Lack of Impulse Control", - pathologies whose common denominator is a primary alteration in serotonergic neurotransmission.

We know that everyone has the potential to become addicted as addiction is based on the normal desire to go through life with less pain and more pleasure. It starts when someone abandons the natural ways of nurturing themselves emotionally, using objects and not people. It is a way of saying: "I don't trust people"; "I don't need to face what I don't wish to"; "I am afraid of facing my life and my problems"; "objects and events are more important than people"; "I can do all I want, whenever I want it, not mattering who gets hurt by it" (even if it is myself).

It is a desperate compromise with a negative lifestyle, but which will provide very short-term pleasures.

Objects of addiction and mood swings

There are numerous potentially addictive objects: alcohol, cigarettes, food, drugs, gambling, sex, etc. The choice of the object of addiction depends on its availability. It is very common for an addict to replace an addictive object with another; for example, replacing alcohol or cigarettes with food. It is also common for a person to be multi-addicted (BLACK, 1990, p. 74). Table 1 exemplifies some addictions and their most common objects:

ADDICTS	OBJECT OF ADDICTION
Alcoholics	Alcohol consumption
Obese people or anorexics	Consumption of huge amounts of food or fasting
Compulsive players	Play games on TV and the Internet
Shoplifters	Small thefts in stores
Sex addicts	Pornography and promiscuity
Compulsive shoppers	Shop with no limits
Compulsive workers	Excessive work

experience the feelings of anxiety, boredom, depression and distress. They run from themselves being occupied with something other than themselves.

TABLE 1 - ADDICTS AND THEIR OBJECTS

What all addictive objects have in common is the fact that they produce a quick and pleasant mood swing, which is typically expressed in one of these three directions:

1. **Excitement**: a hypomanic state where the individual feels all-powerful, omnipotent, and complete.
2. **Satiety:** a relaxed state, full of a sense of being oblivious and anesthetized to pain and distress.
3. **Trance:** an altered state of consciousness that provides the two previous sensations. It is somewhat hypnotic in nature and creates a rewarding virtual reality where one experiences a state of heightened spiritual awareness.

The seductive and addictive factor of an addictive object lies largely in the fact that it produces these mood changes very quickly. If the effect of the addiction were delayed, the addiction would not occur.

Addiction development

Addiction is a process. It has a definite beginning, although its exact origin is often confusing. It goes through various stages of development and comes to a conclusive end (which sometimes coincides with the death of the individual).

Stage I: Internal change

Addiction begins when the addict, as well as all normal individuals, experience a mood change resulting from the object of addiction. The difference is that for the addict, this quick escape from a painful reality causes an impact of immeasurable intensity. It is an illusion, extremely pleasant, of relief and avoidance of the negative feelings. Some gamblers, for example, start to become addicted after the first game in which they won a large amount of money.

From this point, a mental obsession begins to precede and generate the addictive behavior (addictive acting out). For example: studying horse races, going through prostitute-filled streets, going to markets, clothes stores and sales, etc.

In Stage I, the addict behaves within socially acceptable limits. The object of addiction is like a friend who helps the person out in difficult times, throwing them off course and/or curing the pain.

Stage II: lifestyle changes

In the second stage, the addict regularly practices their addiction: drinking, eating, buying, consuming pornography, etc. The addictive behavior becomes ritualized[23], that is, it begins to present a sequence of repetitive acts. Rituals preserve behavior, demanding that everything be done in the right order; otherwise, they have to start all over again. The original personality of an individual (the true self) begins to change and accommodates the addicted personality. People who are related to the addict now realize that something is wrong and, simultaneously, they start to lie to justify or disguise the behavior. Common lies are, for example, hiding food, opening secret accounts, searching for prostitutes, drinking before going home, etc.

Every time they lie, the addict gets more drawn into their own addiction. In the end, they start to blame others and deny fear, shame and the lack of control for their inappropriate behavior.

In this stage, the addiction begins to lose its seductive power. It still helps to avoid the originally felt pain, but it also gradually begins to cause some of its own.

STAGE III - TOTAL LOSS OF CONTROL

In this third stage, the addicted side of the personality gains full control over the "true self," which no longer offers resistance. The well-being once obtained from the object of the addiction succumbs to the

---

23 Rituals reinforce relations with what they represent, deepen the compromise and unite people with the same beliefs. The difference between healthy rituals and addictive ones is that the former connects us to people in the community and do us good; the latter isolate us and end up hurting us. The behavior ritualization offers the comfort of the certainty of achieving the desired change in mood. Each part of the ritual is important as a means of behavior language and escaping the option "drink or not to drink". For example, an alcoholic only needs to pass in front of a bar so that the rest of the ritual that leads to drinking can occur. It is a sort of trance which involves the person and leaves no space for thinking something else or listening to themselves. The addicts are fanatic about their rituals, and usually practice them in solitude or in the company of other addicts.

stress caused by the accumulated lies, interpersonal relationship tensions, and displeasure at the object's absence. The addictive acting out starts to bring more pain than pleasure.

The addict is only able to feel peace and security when involved in their addictive rituals. They avoid any close contact that might reveal their total deterioration. On the other hand, they fear being alone as they are not able to take care of their own life. They start to parasitize family members while manipulating them at the same time to get them to meet their needs and act as their caregivers. They tend to be clingy, insistent, asking for another chance or playing the victim.

Finally, they end up losing jobs and friends, getting in trouble with the law, and reaching financial, health and personal degradation. Gastric problems, sexually transmitted diseases and suicide are common amongst chronic addicts.

Etiology of addictions

The etiology of addictions, as it is comprehended presently, is varied. Some reasons are listed below:

1. Cognitive reasons: lack of information regarding the damage drugs cause; logic and thought disorders.
2. Emotional reasons: related to the development of the patient and their experience of child dependency, various types of abuse, etc.
3. Physiological reasons: alterations in the physiology and functioning of the brain caused by chemical intoxication.
4. Genetic reasons: there are studies about the possible genetic influence in the development of addictions.
5. Philosophical and social reasons: which emphasize the lack of meaning and values in modern life, based on success, lack of time and intimate human relations and existential solitude.

Treatment for addictions

Studies on addiction are pessimistic regarding therapeutic successes. The maximum rate of cure reported is 25%. However, to achieve that, all of the following therapeutic strategies must be used together: 1) Medicative treatment; 2) Attendance at AA meetings; 3) Family psychotherapy; and 4) Individual psychotherapy.

Each intervention removed from this package reduces the chances of success, which is why each will be discussed separately.

1. Antidepressant medication

Depression among addicts is difficult to diagnose initially, especially because many patients come to the office in a good mood, complaining of relationship problems, and rarely acknowledging their addiction as their main problem. Instead, the object of the addiction is perceived as a friend who circumstantially helps and can be sent away when no longer needed.

Depression is masked by this self-medication, which makes it difficult to address. Topics such as the injustices of life, gambling, harassment from others, etc., usually take over discussions during the first sessions. When the drug problem is addressed and abstinence is initiated, emotional chaos occurs and the frequency of depression increases. It entails much patience from the addict and their family and a great deal of consistency from the therapist.

Studies show that many addicts need to "hit rock bottom"; in other words, an extreme experience of destruction of their own life (loss of employment, marriage, or children, being found drunk in the street, being imprisoned for debts, etc.) before they believe that they have no control over their addiction and start wanting to treat it.

These catastrophic experiences are therapeutic because humans often gravitate from a stressful situation to one that is less stressful. Abstinence, at the beginning, is unnatural because it is less satisfying than the high state that the drug provides. It is like asking someone to throw away their most precious jewel.

Only after a person reaches "rock bottom" can this relationship sometimes be reversed and the perception of what is worse changed. The addict becomes frightened by their total decay and wants to do everything within their power to prevent this catastrophic end once again.

The crisis (the "experience of hitting rock bottom") opens up a crack in the delirious protective wall of addictive cognition. It is a rare chance of coming into contact with their true self, but as soon as the crisis passes, the crack heals and the delusional system takes over again. Unfortunately, most addicts' families, wanting to protect their image, cover for the addict, and keep them from living out this self-destructive experience. The goal in working with addicts' families is to help them see that their co-dependence ends up harming more than it helps.

If before abstinence, the patient felt the injustice of their reality and the lack of excitement in life, their dissatisfaction following abstinence will take on macroscopic proportions. Many authors indicate antidepressant medication as the first step in treatment, even before abstinence, believing that it will help the addict tolerate the pain of facing reality. Antidepressants are highly recommended, as they are not addictive. Benzodiazepines, on the other hand, should be avoided as they are addictive, and care must be taken to not replace one addiction with another.

Abstinence is a formidable and very difficult challenge, as it requires:

A. The addict losing their confidence in their ability to control the addiction; they need to know that their sense of reality is distorted, and they cannot rely on themselves. The extreme experience is a painful fall, but it offers a great lesson. The therapist must help the patient reach this conclusion.

B. Addicts give in to perceptions to those of someone else to see if what they perceive truly exists. Addicts must let someone else (spouse, AA leader, therapist, etc.) take control, and this will be especially difficult for those who were brought up in a dysfunctional environment that led them in the opposite direction.

3. AA (Alcoholics Anonymous)

Addicts confuse and seduce normal people with their addictive logic. Hence, homogeneous group therapy is especially important, as it requires "a confrontation between equals." This is the first among the various therapeutic factors described below, responsible for AA worldwide success:

1. It enables the individual to see him/herself reflected in the members of the group, as in a mirror, which can be extremely therapeutic because it allows others to point out aspects about the addict to which they cannot admit themselves.

2. The absence of upper/lower hierarchies and the fact that everyone in the group shares the same addiction and the same shame for intra-family abusive experiences facilitates the approach to the problem itself: "I am one of many, not the weak one in the group". It also favors the recognition of family values and dispels the myths that stimulate the addiction. For example: a man is only a man if he drinks or having things is having love, etc.

3. AA's twelve-step philosophy postulates the spiritual power of a superior, protective, and wise entity (it can be God, nature, health, etc.). This spiritual bias is critical in addressing the "basic insecurity of the addict," who is naturally suspicious of other humans and of themselves. During the first meetings, the attendees must recognize that they do not have control over their disease, but that a higher being does, and that being will help them.

4. AA's notion of time – "You live one day at a time" and "Just for today I will not use the object of my addiction" - perfectly caters to the enormous difficulty the addict has in delaying gratification. His emotional logic contains only the present, the now! This altered concept of time goes along with the familiar argument: "I can stop whenever I want." In fact, it is possible. All addicts are experts in stopping a million times, making new resolutions for their lives, and resuming the addiction once again. It is a vicious cycle that can continue for years;

5. The group supports relapses and welcomes restarts, always a difficult situation to face when one has to overcome an addiction;

6. Finally, AA assists in the breakdown of addictive rituals and encourages the fact that certain locations should be avoided at certain times; for example, bars, bingo halls, shops, being left alone at night at home[24], etc.

---

24 Most obese, bulimic and compulsive people eat at night and hidden, without anyone seeing.

4 - Family psychotherapy and/or support groups for addicts' families

Families of addicts often indirectly stimulate the use of drugs and harbor dysfunctional, co-dependent relational psychodynamics, which can cause a great deal of suffering. Drug use may, for example, be encouraged by family habits that are apparently trivial, such as: excessive use of self-medication, social drinking, smoking, use of caffeine as a stimulant, using food for emotional gratification and comfort, overworking, etc. Children and young people grow up watching adults seek relief from their conflicts and pain with these practices, and this can create future models of conduct in which the children seek to engage.

Moreover, being with addicted individuals can be quite destructive to one's psyche and requires specific support measures. AA includes groups that support family members of alcoholics and addicts. These are Al-Anon (for family members and friends of alcoholics) and Nar-Anon (groups for addicted people's families in Brazil). In these groups, they learn to deal with the psychodynamics of codependency. Their fundamental teachings are:

- No one is responsible for the disease of another person, nor for his/her recovery.
- One should not suffer because of someone else's actions and reactions.
- One should not allow oneself to be used or abused in the interests of another person's recovery.
- One should not do for others what they should do for themselves.
- One should not manipulate situations so that others eat, sleep, get up, pay the bills, or do not drink.
- One should not cover up the mistakes or sloppiness of another person.
- One should not create a crisis.
- One should not prevent a crisis, if the latter is in the natural course of events.

Families are monitored to detect the presence of a certain emotional detachment to protect themselves and allow the addict to try to "hit rock bottom," the extreme experience that can possibly help overcome the addiction. Topics such as loyalty, shame, guilt, and secrets, are shared within the groups, and the results are normally very good.

5. Individual psychotherapy

It is not easy to therapeutically approach addicted people because of the impenetrability of this mindset dominated by a logical and biased way of thinking and because of the changes in the conception of time.

What we achieve, in general, is an apparent improvement at first, followed by a relapse and abandonment of therapy. I worked once with an obese man who lost 70 pounds in three years of individual psychotherapy, only to recover them all back in two months and leave the treatment at the end. Preventing relapses must be a constant concern from the very beginning of therapy.

We believe that psychotherapists who care for addicted people need to be humble enough to admit that they cannot deal with the problem alone. The pleasure that the drug provides is much more enticing than one hour per week of reflective work. The advice of a psychiatrist and the inclusion of AA are necessary, at least at some point, for both the patient and their family to successfully complete therapy.

The seductive role of "savior of the world" should also be avoided at all costs and should not be the controller of drug intake, diet, expenses, etc. to prevent being taken in by the codependent psychodynamics and losing one's operability. These are issues and practices that can be discussed in psychotherapy, but it is not the therapist's function to control them.

Winning the trust of the addict is the first step, and they should be warned that they would feel a great deal of discomfort during psychotherapy. In addition, they should be made aware that they may have to be medicated and, at some point, need to attend AA. If the patient does not agree to these conditions, it is preferable to not accept this person into psychotherapy and to keep "the only remaining bullet" for another time when they really want to be treated.

The psychodynamics of addictions: the true self ("I") *versus* addicted self-addicted part of the personality)

In working with addicts during psychotherapy, the therapist must understand that two client personalities are present at all times: one that wants to collaborate ("I") and the other that surreptitiously seeks to boycott, lie, and end any effort to push them away from drugs (the addicted side).

The addiction process either starts randomly or as a result of some discomfort. The object or addictive practice creates a sense of well-being or perfection—at least for a while. The "I" feels guilty and anxious. These are initial warning signs that, unfortunately, fail to inspire action over time.

Every time the addiction acts, the addicted personality gains a little more control. The "I" disapproves of this way of acting, feeling and thinking, but it loves the mood change that the addictive object provides. It promises to control the addict with its willpower and sometimes succeeds, but it eventually succumbs to the addicted personality.

The "I" gradually becomes less tolerant of the discomfort, and any frustration is experienced as pain, thus signaling the need to seek out the object of the addiction.

Addiction is the denial of emotional pain and a refusal to depend on the help of other human beings for relief. The addict does not care for their wife or children, or even for themselves, ignoring they can get sick or even die. The addicted self-dreams of escaping pain, obtaining peace, sensory perfection and immediate gratification; while the "I" dreams of controlling the addict. Until the "I" starts losing energy, eventually giving up and surrendering.

It is a vicious cycle: the more the "I" seeks relief in the addiction, the more shame and guilt they feels and the more they undervalue themselves, which increases the pain and initial discomfort. Then, once again, they seek relief in their addictive practices, and the cycle resumes. Figure 1 illustrates this process:

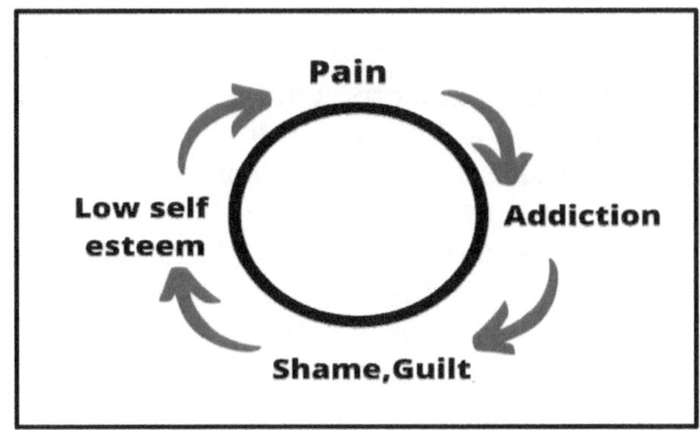

FIGURE 1 - THE VICIOUS CIRCLE OF ADDICTION

For psychotherapy to be effective, the patient has to understand this cycle and realize that they have no control over the addiction. The addicted side is much stronger and articulated, and even in abstention will prove a threat to the self.

Psychodrama and addictions[25]

Studies of traumatized animals and patients (MARY, 2004; VAN DER KOLK, MCFARLANE and WEISAETH, 1996) suggest that experiential psychotherapies are more effective than just verbal therapies.

The immediate response to a stressful situation[26] triggers reaction mechanisms of the sympathetic nervous system, known as an "alert reaction." The animal organism gets ready for fight or flight, breathing becomes deeper, the blood flows from the stomach and intestines to the heart and to the muscles, the ongoing processes in the digestive system cease, sugar is released from the liver's reserves, the spleen twitches and releases its contents, the hypophysis stimulates the adrenal glands and the body is flooded with hormones, like adrenaline. That is an efficient preparation for activity and combat, as Walter Cannon already described in 1939 and Paul MacLean reaffirmed in 1952.

---

25 This text is a duplicate of the text on pages 50-53
26 A stressful situation means any situation that leads the individual to a state of despair, whether they are fighting to preserve their lives or that of someone meaningful to them.

Levine (1999) shows us that when an animal is hindered from reacting, archaic brain mechanics start operating, the reptilian brain, provoking a freezing of the vital functions, thus simulating death in life. Through this trickery, pretending to be dead, the animal may succeed in being left by the predator or at least, to gain time to think of another escape strategy.

The same occurs, with some differences, to the human animal. In 1952, the American neurologist Paul MacLean described the three folded nature of the human brain, a result of our phylogenetic evolution (see Figure 2).

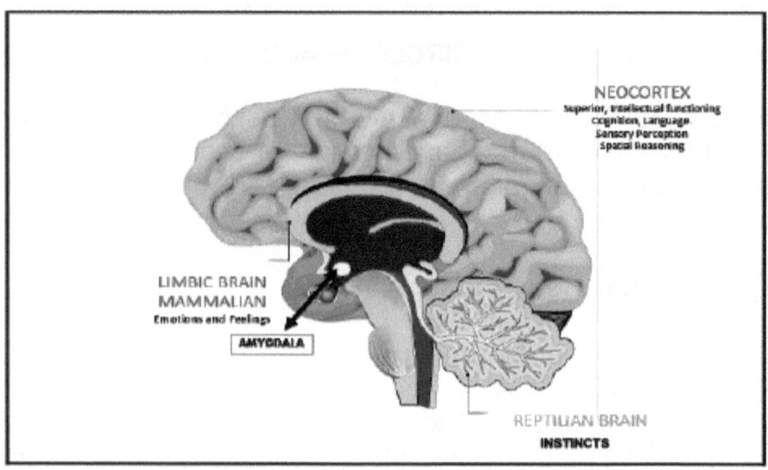

FIGURE 2 - PAUL MACLEAN, "THE VISCERAL BRAIN" (1952).

The brainstem is the primitive, reptilian brain. It is residual of our prehistoric past, useful for quick decisions that do not demand much thinking. The reptilian brain focuses on survival, and it is driven by fear, going into action whenever we are in danger and do not have time to think. In a world where the fittest survive, the reptilian brain is concerned with getting food and not becoming food.

The central layer of the brain is the limbic part or mammalian brain, the root of emotions, humor and feelings. The neocortex is the most evolutionarily advanced part of the brain. It controls our ability to speak, think and solve problems. The neocortex affects creativity and the ability to learn and covers approximately 80% of the brain.

The human brain, although being more specialized, does not fully functional in traumatic situations (LE DOUX, 1996; VAN DER KOLK, 1996), as the neocortex undergoes functional alterations releasing hormones that make it numb (see Figure 3). The memories kept at this moment do not need to be verbalized, they are formed by sensations, visual images and motor patterns, as language is a neocortical function.

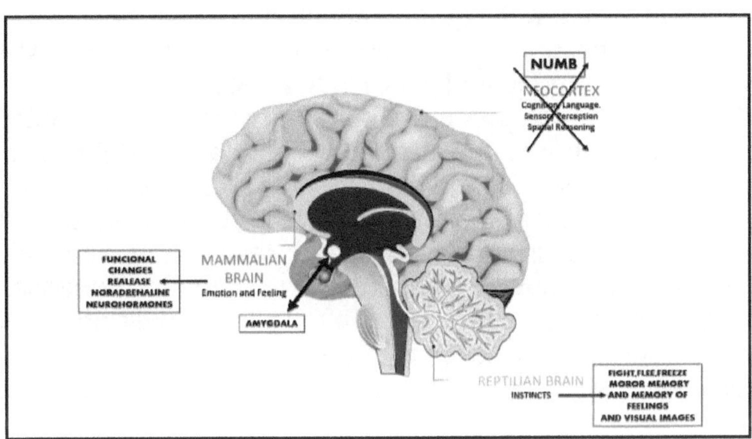

FIGURE 3 - BRAIN AND MEMORY FUNCTIONING IN POST-TRAUMATIC STRESS

Similar to animals, human beings work with the reptilian brain when prevented from reacting. Freezing of vital functions is shown through superficial breathing and stiff muscles, simulating *rigor mortis* and an anesthetized mind, as in an ethereal state. However, contrary to the animal - which, after the danger has passed, defrosts through a noticeable body shivering - the human being intermediates these physical functions with thoughts, feelings, emotions, invisible loyalties, etc., which are results from the other two parts of the brain he/she has.

Many times, a person who was raped, for example, conceals their horror, refrains from crying, shaking, and feeling ashamed to pretend to the world that nothing has happened. As a result of this non-action, their body will not recover from the trauma and the helplessness experienced at the moment they were attacked.

The individual lacks an offensive action and retaking control, which are often only attained many years later, through the active repetition of the violence or abuse - this time taking the role of the abuser or of someone who holds control (many addictions are disastrous attempts to simulate control).

Dramatization allows this missing action to come about, enabling muscles to produce a safe discharge of the body's need for control recovery. I would like to remind you that psychodrama was one of the first body therapies, and Moreno (1992, v.1, p. 187) already said that the body remembers what the mind forgets, especially events that take place in early childhood, even before language acquisition. The best way to recover memory from actions is through expressive methods, which address the whole person (body and mind) in the action.

It should also be added that psychodrama, which is an existential and relational approach, offers the patient a chance of establishing a meaningful and trustful human connection, instead of using the object of addiction. Through a dialectical movement - which researches both the patient's relational wound in their past and their characterological defenses, and the here and now of a continent and validating relationship - psychodrama is a very adept resource for illuminating and discriminating the different characters and processes in struggle within the addict. Some real cases[27] will now be described illustrating the use of psychodrama with addictions.

In interviews

Most clients who come to us do not know what psychodrama is, and many do not even know what psychotherapy is. It is quite likely that the vast majority of lay people think that they should just spend some time with us and tell us about their lives so we can provide them with solutions to their most intimate problems. In addition, some clients are afraid of our profession because we are either seen as wizards who can read souls, or as arrogant people who feel superior to others.

I believe we need to help our patients know who we are, build their confidence in what we do, as well as help them to become familiar with our working tools. Trust and knowledge are constructed gradually, which is why we conduct at least three interviews before accepting a client into a psychotherapy contract.

---

27 All the patients' names are fictitious. We are going to use "T" and the fictitious initial of the patient's name designates, respectively, therapist and patient in the mentioned examples.

I conduct one or two verbal interviews, a social atom - that introduces psychodrama to the patient - and a feedback interview where we summarize our opinion and establish the contract regarding what will be worked on. We specifically perform, with the addicted patient, when possible, three different social atoms in addition to the verbal interviews: 1) a traditional social atom (Figure 4); 2) a social atom during the addiction (Figure 5); 3) a familiar addiction atom, or a genogram of the addictions (Figure 6).

GOALS
- Explore the sociometric context in which the client is inserted and train for future dramatizations. It is important to know who their natural auxiliary egos are, who can support them if depression or any other more serious disorder happens, and also what sociometric spaces are lacking in their social atom. Sometimes you see an adult person surrounded by the primary family, but without friends, as if he/she were still a child in the care of his family.

- A – After a brief non-specific warm-up, preferably on the move, such as walking, stretching, etc., a cushion, chair or stool is placed in the center of the room, representing the client.

- B – The client is asked to show the most important relationships in his current life and to place them in an order of proximity according to the affective importance they have. Ex.: target shooting.

- C – The client is asked to step into his/hers role and realize how he/she feels, at the center of those relationships. What changes need to be made to make them feel happier.

- D – Next, the client is asked (from his own role) to tell the first person who was specified what his/hers relationship with her is like. We can make an emotional suggestion, such as: If you had to say a sentence from your heart to this person, what would you say?

- E – Afterwards, it is suggested that the client change roles and assume the role of each of the people he/she has mentioned. The important thing is to do a brief warm-up, through an interview, to help the client to incorporate the different roles. Ex: What is your name? How old are you? How are you physically? What do you think of my client? Tell him/her today what you don't normally say but think about him/her?

- F – If the protagonist has many characters, he is asked to choose among the main ones.

FIGURE 4 - TRADITIONAL SOCIAL ATOM

OBJECTIVES: TO EXPLORE THE SOCIOMETRIC CONTEXT OF THE TIME OF ADDICTION, WHO ARE THE AUXILIARY EGOS THAT SEDUCE AND SUPPORT THE PRACTICE OF ADDICTION. IT IS IMPORTANT FOR CLIENTS TO UNDERSTAND HOW THEIR SOCIAL LANDSCAPE CHANGES WHEN THEY DECIDE TO USE DRUGS AND WHAT HAPPENS TO THEIR RELATIONAL ATOM PRIOR TO DRUGS.

a) After a brief non-specific warm-up, preferably on the move, such as walking, stretching, etc., a cushion, chair or stool is placed in the center of the room, representing the client.

b) Clients are asked to show their relationships when taking drugs or when practicing addiction. And, further, that they order these relationships in order of proximity, according to the influence they exert on their addition. You can give the example of target shooting again, and show how this is done with the pads.

c) The clients are asked to step into their own roles and realize how they feel at the center of those relationships. You can also ask them to look at their original social atom (minimized in a corner of the room) and watch what changes have taken place.

d) The clients, are asked from their own role to tell the first person who has been specified what their relationship are like. We can make an emotional suggestion, like, if you had to say a sentence from your heart to this person, what would you say?

e) Then, it is suggested that the client change roles and assume the tole of each of the people in question. The important thing is to do a brief warm-up, through an interview, to help them to incorporate the different roles. For example: What is your name, how old are you, how are you physically? What do you think of my client? Tell him today what you don't normally say but think about him?

If the protagonist has many characters, he is asked to choose among the main ones. Many other questions can be addressed to the characters, according to the aspects the therapist wants to investigate. It is important to observe not only the verbal material obtained through this resource, but also the patient's entire body attitude, the distances defined by him and the subtleties of the personalities of the different characters he reveals. Drawing a picture of the addicted social atom in the client's protocol can be very helpful.

FIGURE 5- SOCIAL ATOM DURING ADICTION

GENOGRAM

Objectives: to investigate the presence of addictive habits, compulsive and/or abusive, which act as shame generators in the client's family atom.

Datasheet: The client is asked to rate, on a scale from 1 to 10, the presence of the following behaviors observed by a family member: addictions (drink, drugs, shopping, food, work, etc.); perfectionism; procrastination[28]; anger; victimization, depression, compulsion, suicide or any other dysfunctional habit.

Both the social atom during the addiction, as well as the genogram of addictions, help the therapist and client to focus on the extent of damage and family influence. They also help to prevent a relapse, as they materialize in an obvious manner, people and situations the addict must avoid if they do not want to fall back on addiction.

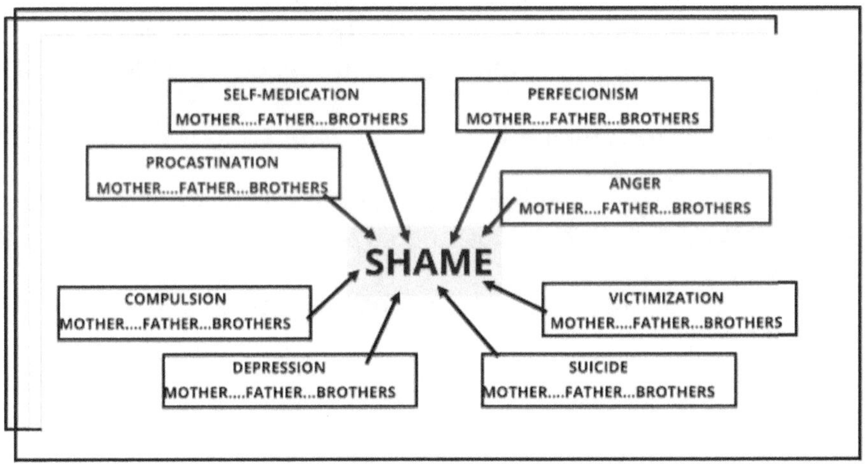

FIGURE 6 - GENOGRAM OF ADDICTIONS

---

28 Procrastinate: the habit of always leaving tasks for later that should be done now.

At the beginning of therapy: differentiating the self and the addict

1.Using masks

V., 35 years old, divorced, obese, with two children, owns a company that is facing serious administrative problems. She complains about nocturnal bulimia[29] crises, which she cannot control. On these occasions, she devours everything that appears in front of her, whether savory, sweet, fruity, ice-cream, etc. "These are moments of gastronomic madness," she says. "I put on all the weight I lost previously when on a diet and doing exercise."

In the first few sessions, T (the therapist) said she wanted to work on[30] "this crazy fat lady that appears late at night." T asked her to imagine the scene in which this "crazy fat lady" last appeared. She set up the scene in her home kitchen the night before. She was alone, looking inside the fridge and in the cupboard for anything she could eat.

After the detailed kitchen scene set-up, T asked her to begin her soliloquy, one minute before she went to the kitchen:

V. (in soliloquy, one minute before) - *I'm sad, alone, and afraid of what will happen tomorrow* (referring to a serious problem in the company).

T. - Okay. Now, continue the soliloquy, but go to the kitchen until the "crazy fat lady" appears.

V - (in soliloquy): *I want to sleep, switch off, and not think about tomorrow.* At this moment, she stops and says to T. - *The "crazy fat lady" begins to open the fridge.*

T. - Very good! Freeze a little and choose a mask with which to be this "crazy fat lady."

---

29 *Bulimia nervosa*: is essentially characterized by the presentation of binge eating and inappropriate compensatory methods to prevent weight gain (purging, fasting, or exaggerated exercise). Furthermore, the self-assessment of individuals with bulimia nervosa is excessively influenced by body shape and weight.
30 It is useful to ask at the beginning of the sessions what the patients want to work on that day. They usually answer and with that are stimulated to develop their autonomy and responsibility during the time we spend together.

V. goes to the wall where the masks are hanging and carefully takes down a chubby face with red cheeks and a feather on top of the head and says: *This is the one, without a doubt!*

T. - *Wear it for a while and imagine this scene: V. is alone, worried, and sad. She goes to the refrigerator* (T puts down a cushion to mark the role of the client), *and then you show up, enter the scene, and talk with V.*

V. (with the mask on, in the role of the crazy fat lady) - *I came to help you, dear* (in an exaggerated way). *I'm your dear friend. I always fill you up with something and make you sleep. Come, and I'll sing you a lullaby.*

T. - *Change places for a while, take off the mask* (T. puts the mask on the pillow, and V. assumes her proper place at the refrigerator door).

V. (as V., towards the "crazy fat lady") - *Get away from me, you don't help me. I need to lose weight to change my life, and you don't let me. I'm still fat and alone. Go away. I hate you!*

After a few more role reversals to deepen the characteristics of V.'s split aspects, T. asks V. to leave the scene and watch while T. sets two pillows, one with the mask and one without, and quickly repeats the dialogue (so that the patient does not lose her warm-up). Then, T. says: "These two parts are yours, V. One brings you to therapy, and the other offers you the addiction. We need to know them better, and we will do so from now on."

2. Executing doubles of the addict part

It is very useful to run doubles of the addicted side, especially emphasizing the paradoxical nature of this side of the personality.

Crazy fat lady - *Bring me your pain, and I'll give you relief.*

T. (as a double of V. in the role of the crazy fat lady): *Bring me your pain, and I will give you the illusion of relief.*

Crazy fat lady - *I shall set you free.*

T. (as a double of V. in the role of the crazy fat lady): *I will be your only boss.*

Crazy fat lady - *Spend some time with me. You can trust me. You can trust no one else.*

T. (as the double of V. in the role of the crazy fat lady) - *Spend some time with me, and I'll teach you not to trust anyone.*

Crazy fat lady: - *I'll teach you a way to not face your problems.*

T. (as the double of V. in the role of the crazy fat lady) - *You will get rid of the problems for a short time, but they will not go away.*

Over time, T. may propose that the client takes on the double role of the addicted side herself, to internalize a type of reasoning that is less influenced by the addicted logic.

3. Writing letters

Writing letters is a good way of discriminating between parts - those of the writer and the reader. It is an excellent strategic resource for maintaining the warming up between sessions. In the case of addiction, we may suggest that the letters be written in several ways:

- From the addicted side to the self.
- From the self to the addicted side.
- From the body to the addicted side.
- From the object of addiction to the self.
- From various members of the social atom to the self.
- From the addicted side to the closest family relationships, etc.

Building metaphors for the addicted part

W., a 42-year-old, homosexual, highly successful professional, has a partner with whom he has lived for 20 years. He's a "sex addict," with eventual compulsions to go out late at night and have sexual intercourse with strangers without using protective measures.

"Like a vampire hunting for blood," he says spontaneously, referring to this ego-dystonic part of his personality. The therapist asks him to forget himself and to play the vampire role, telling his story, with a beginning, a middle and an end.

"I was a handsome young man," he says, "when one night, walking casually down the street, I was attacked and bitten by a vampire. I lost the freedom to be who I wanted to be, and I transformed into a vampire. Being a vampire is not a choice. It is my destiny." The therapist then asks him to show, with his body, how he felt as a vampire. He shrinks and says: "Ashamed". The therapist gets closer, puts her hand on his back, and asks him, "When else have you ever felt so ashamed?" "When my father beat me in front of everybody", he says, referring to a scene that occurred when he was five years old.

Often, throughout his psychotherapy, we worked on this scene to understand the vampire side of his personality. As you can see, metaphors are great resources with which to bring out split worlds - parts not assumed of the life story and of the clients' selves. They allow multiple therapeutic uses and can be brought forward spontaneously, as in the cited example, or built by implementing some behaviors, feelings, etc.

The empty chair

The therapist places an empty chair in front of the patient and suggests to him to imagine there are people sitting there, or parts of himself with whom he wishes to work. In the case of the addiction, the drug itself can be embodied there, as well as the partners of the addiction, the addicted side of the personality that dominates the self, metaphors, dreams, etc.

The role-playing is done with the client changing positions, i.e., the client plays one role, then he/she changes chairs and play the other; they act out roles without dramatic action. This technique can be used as an initial warm-up, followed by open stage work, or as a single technique within a psychodramatic work.

It is interesting to ask the patient to talk to the drug, reversing the roles and, after some time, becoming the double of this object or addictive practice to externalize the unsaid, the future consequence. And thus, to finally be able to appropriate the experience itself and not dissociate and forget it.

The therapist may play roles as well, if he/she wishes, or he/she can merely observe, interviewing both conflicting parties and presenting a point of view that has not been addressed so far.

C. (40 years old; smokes marijuana all day in the car, at work, at school, etc.) to the empty chair, where marijuana sits - *I need you.*

C. (as marijuana to C.) - *Me too. We are an inseparable pair.*

C. (to marijuana) - *But I'm not going to my classes and may lose my job.*

C. (as marijuana to C.) - *Well, that's what they say. We understand things better, more deeply.*

C. (to marijuana) - *No way, I do not even remember what I have to write today. I have to ask Luis.*

C. (as marijuana to C.) - *That idiot nerd…*

T. asks C. to stand up, places a cushion in the place of C., and says, "Now I'll be marijuana and you stay behind me, explaining what I, marijuana, am not saying."

T. (as marijuana to cushion representing C.) - *Luis is an idiot. He looks stupid. He doesn´t know anything.*

C. (as marijuana double) – *Just stay with me. I'm your only friend. Don't study. Don't date. You´ll only be happy with me.*

C. (as C., to T.) - *It is just like my mom, who does not like any of my girlfriends. It seems she wants to hold me down.*

T. then asks C. to construct a recent scene in which his mother showed this domineering aspect, and the session continues with a classic scene montage, using typical psychodrama techniques.

There are many ways to promote the discrimination of these parts that are in conflict, and we find it extremely useful to spend some time of the therapy session processing this division.

Entering the patient's psychodynamics: working with a regressive scene

The psychotherapeutic work is not complete if the client is not responsible for his way of reacting to the frustrations of life and does not stop blaming his relationships for his misadventures. Addict patients, with their fallacious false logic, are usually seen as victims from the world (parents, work colleagues, etc.) and claim to use the drug because of it.

Arguing rationally, as we've already seen, gets nowhere. What should we do to creatively surprise the client and perhaps manage to enter this addicted psychodynamics, which always leads to drugs and impotence?

For me, intrapsychic psychodrama, with regressive or infantile scenes, is what most helps us in this arduous task, as it allows the director to start a dramatization exactly in the client's current impotence to, little by little, begin to understand when and why this impotence was raised. The client is not forced to understand anything, no change of conduct is required, we just follow their associations from other moments when impotence was also present.

In the case of addictions, it is a powerful therapeutic resource to discriminate childhood pain and defenses from more adult solutions to issues with the same emotional impact, as well as to assess the role of the client's current addictive behavior in his/her life history.

In my book Emotional Survival - Childhood Pain Relived in the Drama of Adult Life (1998), there is a whole chapter dedicated to the child nuclear scene and here, in this same book, in the chapter "Steps for using successful dramatization", I also describe, didactically, this handling. See the following example:

T. (to A.) - *Go around the room, stretch your body, and start thinking of when you felt this urge most recently.*

A.   - *Yesterday, after walking in the morning.*

T. - *Where were you?*

A. - *When the urge started?*

T. - *Yes.*

A. - *I was combing my hair after my shower.*

T. - *We will set up your bathroom, the mirror ... Where is the door of this room?*[31]

A. provides the locations of all the bathroom parts, the cabinet, mirror, etc.

T. - *Begin to comb, and start a soliloquy.*

A. - *Today I am well, I should fit into those leather pants... I need to buy them. If I go to the store, I can pay in ten installments, I can even wear them tonight to C's party.*

T. - *Take a deep breath, close your eyes and go into in yourself. Look for what you feel in your body when you start to think about it.*

A. - *My hands shake and sweat, I get excited.*

T. - *Let this excitement take over your whole body.*

A. Starts jumping, higher and higher, laughing...

T. - *Very good. Higher. Jump higher... What does this joy remind you of?*

A. (Immediately) - *My father coming to take me every two weeks. I would wait at the door, we would go to the restaurant, bowling, or shopping. He bought everything I wanted. He had more money than my mother. My mother even used to tell me to ask him for things.*

---

31 It is good to start the construction of the scene by the front door of the place where it happens. It helps to define the space and warms up the patient, since he/she realizes the therapist really knows where the furniture, windows, etc. are.

T. - *Any day in particular?*

A. - *Many similar days. I had a father every two weeks.*

T. - *We will set up one of those days here ... Remember a moment* from one of those days.

A. - *Buying a car game* (an expensive motor car race). *It was a big toy store there at the top of Lapa* (a district in SãoW Paulo). *We had already been there, in another week... We went in the morning, on Saturday. Then, we set it up at his house, we set it up all afternoon. We were very happy.*

T. - *A., take a deep breath and close your eyes. Picture this scene inside you, and especially look at your face, your body, and your age. What are your emotions right now?*

A. - *Joy. Joy!*

T. - *What did you need at this point in your life?*

A. - *I needed this time not to end and for it not to be so rare* (he cries). *He died when I was 12, and the two weeks were over.*

T. - *Take a deep breath and go back to the scene within you... What are you learning at this time in your life that you will never forget?*

C. - *I like my father, even though my mother did not* (crying). *He is good to me. He likes playing with me* (more crying).

T. (Going to the corner where he left the bathroom scene and the shopping urge minimized): *Look at this 35-year-old man here... He needs to go to this store to buy this expensive object... Do you have something to say to him - your nine-year-old self, this very minute?*

A. - *Your father is not there, you idiot* (crying)... *You will only get into trouble.*

T. - *Go back to your adult role, A., in front of the mirror. Look for a minute at this boy...* (points to the childhood scene in which the cushions mark the roles). *Do you think you could get in touch with him during the week, write him a short letter? I feel that you need to talk. It seems that there is some relationship between your father and the car game, the urge, the leather pants, the fancy store... Think about it, and we will continue in the next session.*

In the next session, warmed up by the note that the client, in his adult role, wrote to his boy self, we resume his father's death scene. The patient, aged 12, is in front of his father's coffin, sad and angry, because his mother and his stepmother have created a tense atmosphere at the funeral.

T. (to A.) - *What do you need at this point in your life?*

A. - *For my mother to stop thinking only about herself and think of me, be with me.*

T. - *What do you learn by not having what you needed?*

A. - *I have to be on my own from now, nobody will care for me.*

T. - *What does this mean for a 12-year-old boy?*

A. - *That I have to look for a way to make money and give myself all I want.*

A. (to T., out of the childhood role and speaking as an adult): *Buying all I want is a way to do this, isn't it?*

T. - *It seems so. Buying all you want represents having a father within yourself, and this is what we need to change.*

End of psychotherapy: setting new behaviors and a new sociometry

The addictive behavior is a safe behavioral and predictable mode of preservation, but it is dysfunctional and uncreative. Psychodrama can do much to develop the spontaneity of the patient to help them train new behaviors and risk themselves in new sociometrics.

Techniques such as role-playing, dramatization of feared scenes and dramatic games help to reveal fears an individual might not otherwise be aware of, behaviors not developed, and roles not played.

We like setting up the office as a privileged and magical laboratory, where pigeons and colorful scarves come out of a black top hat and are later transformed into new dreams, future projects, and new relationships.

Final word: relapse

Relapses in addiction are absolutely normal. The therapist should inform the client that he/she is already expecting this and that he/she will certainly never stop helping him. There is a tendency, almost generalized, for patients to end the therapeutic process following relapse. This is because in addition to being disappointed with the therapy, their self-esteem is very low. They have catastrophic thoughts of personal ruin, which in turn lead back to the cycle of addiction.

Therapists need to pay attention to relapse situations because they are often repeated and because we can predict them if we watch for some indicators. These are some signs the client may show of a possible relapse: skipping therapy, showing remorse and shame, starting to blame others for their problems, self-victimizing, staying slow and repetitive, etc.

Those who relapse do not restart from zero, because they have already made some progress and need only to resume control. Making a prognosis of relapses early in the treatment and paying attention to life situations that may encourage them can shorten the retaking of the control process. Returning to AA is also very difficult the second time, especially for the group shame it brings and because it discredits the therapeutic capacity of the meetings. Individual therapy needs to focus on improving this process of restarting group meetings.

It is desirable for the therapist to share his/her own mistakes because it can act as a model for the patient. "If my doctor or therapist makes mistakes, apologizes and starts all over again, I can too." Errors do not demolish a person. The best thing is to admit them promptly and fix them as soon as possible so that the denials and lies do not accumulate.

Recovery

Recovering from an addiction is to break the dependence of the internal addictive ritual and discover a new way of living, one that is more vulnerable to fears, conflicts, and relationships. Changing the self-image is one of the most difficult aspects of the therapeutic process, and the shame for actions committed in the past can ruin recovery. The therapist must help the client transform shame into guilt, which will then generate remedial action.

Learning to admit mistakes is one of the goals of therapy. It is useful to reframe what clients understand by human nature telling them that to be "human" is to make mistakes and to seek to get it right the next time. Moreover, our admitted vulnerability generates a secondary benefit, which is to encourage empathy from other people and bring them closer to us. Omnipotent people who know everything and do not need help from anyone else, in general, are lonely. We connect with other humans through our very human faults.

REFERENCES
ASSOCIATION, American Psychiatric (1994)- DSM IV: Diagnostic and Statistical Manual of Mental Disorders.
BLACK, Claudia. Double duty: food addicted. Denver: Mac Publishing, 1990.

BLUM, K.; NOBLE, E. SMITH, S.; UHL, G. Substance abuse vulnerability and D2 receptor genes. Trend in Neurosciences, v.16, n.3, p.83-8, 1993.

BRADSHAW, John. Healing the shame that binds you. Rio de Janeiro: Rosa dos Ventos, 1997.

BUSTOS, Dalmiro M. Danger, love at sight. São Paulo: Aleph, 1990.

__________. Novos rumos em psicodrama. São Paulo, Editora Ática, 1992.

__________. Wings and roots. In: Holmes, Paul; Karp, Marcia & Watson, Michael, 1994.Psycodrama since Moreno. No Brasil, publicada por Leituras 2 – Companhia do Teatro Espontâneo.

CANNON, Walter. The Wisdom of the Body. New York: Birmingham, Ala: Classics of Medicine Library, 1994.

CUKIER, Rosa (2008) Emotional Survival: Childhood Pain Relived in the Drama of Adult Life, Lulu.com.

DAYTON, Tian. Trauma and addiction. Ending the cycle of pain through emotional literacy. Florida: Health Communications Inc., 2000.

ERIKSON, E. (1950), Childhood and society. W.W. Norton & Company, New York.

FRANKL, Viktor E. (1998). Man's Search for Meaning: The classic tribute to hope from the Holocaust, Rider, London.

KRAL, V. A.; MACLEAN, Paul A. A triune concept of the brain and behavior. Toronto: Mental Health Foundation by University of Toronto Press, 1973.

LE DOUX, Joseph. The emotional brain: the mysterious underpinnings of emotional life. Rio de Janeiro: Objetiva, 1996.

LEVINE, Peter A. Waking the tiger: healing trauma. São Paulo: Summus, 1999.

WYLIE, M. S. (2004) The limits of talk. Psychotherapy Networker. January/February.

MELLAN, Olivia. Overcoming overspending. New York: Walker and Company, 1995.

PERAZZO, S. (1994). Ainda e sempre psicodrama. São Paulo, Ágora.

PITZELE, P. (1992). "Adolescents, Inside Out: an overview". In: Karp, Marcia & Holmes, Psychodrama – Inspiration and technique, Tavistock / Routledge.

TWERSTI, Abraham J.; NAKKEN, Craig. Addictive thinking and the addictive personality. New York: MJF Books, 1999.

VAN DER KOLK, B.; MCFARLANE, A. WEISAETH L. Traumatic Stress: the effects of overwhelming experience on mind, body and society. New York: Guilford Press, 1996.

YALOM, D. I. The Yalom reader: selections from the work of a master therapist and storyteller. New York: Basic Books, 1998.

STEPS FOR USING SUCCESSFUL DRAMATIZATION32

My objective in this text is to describe, step by step, how I perform the assistance in bipersonal psychodrama, from interviews to the montage and working with regressive scenes.

I have long observed - since my role as teacher and supervisor - that part of the difficulties that young therapists attribute to the "difficult client who does not accept dramatization", is in fact, their own self struggle with the technique and how to use it, not knowing how to initiate the treatment in a didactic way and how to carry on with it safely and technically.

Stimulated by the wonderful questions of my students, I started to create syntheses, summary sheets, tables, drawings, everything I could to make my ideas and my practice clearer. I hope these systematizations are useful to those who seek to develop their role as a psychotherapist. I will develop my ideas on seven topics described below:

1. How to establish a therapeutic relationship that facilitates later psychodramatic practice: contract (time, place, price, replacements); interviews, patients who do not want to dramatize, etc.

2. How to help the client – he/she and not the therapist - to choose, focus and deepen a theme and whether it is better to use an open scene psychodrama or an internal psychodrama.

3. Warming up and warming up maintenance, in an open scene psychodrama.

4. Working with the initial scene, connecting transferential scenes and how to articulate time - present, past, and future - in the dramatization.

5. Deciding which psychodramatic technique to use.

6. Psychodrama with regressive scene - the adult's inner child.

7. How to end and manage dramatization when time runs out in the middle of a role play.

I. How to establish a therapeutic relationship that facilitates later psychodramatic practice

---

32 Article published in the book by VASCONCELOS, M. C. (2004)." **Quando a terapia trava"**. São Paulo: Ágora, 2007.

Most clients who come to us do not know what psychodrama is, and many do not even know what psychotherapy is. It is quite likely that the vast majority of lay people think that they should just spend some time with us and tell us about their lives so we can provide them with solutions to their most intimate problems. In addition, some clients are afraid of our profession because we are either seen as wizards who can read souls, or as arrogant people who feel superior to others.

I believe we need to help our patients know who we are, build their confidence in what we do, as well as help them to become familiar with our working tools. Trust and knowledge are constructed gradually, which is why we conduct at least three interviews before accepting a client into a psychotherapy contract.

I conduct one or two verbal interviews, a social atom - that introduces psychodrama to the patient - and a feedback interview where we summarize our opinion and establish the contract regarding what will be worked on. I usually tell clients that I must get to know them to know if I can help them and they must know me, to judge if they really want to open their intimacy to me. I answer all the questions clients ask me and I ask everything I need to assess whether this is a case of psychotherapy alone, whether or not you will need psychiatric coverage, or whether early family therapy would not be a better strategy, etc.

In the first interview, I listen to the client's complaint to understand what their pain is. There are people who talk a lot without, however, letting us see what they truly want a therapeutic process for. In these cases, I ask the client directly: where or what hurts you? It's amazing how this simple question tends to set off the emotion and have a simple, straightforward answer as well. (Figure 1).

As you can see, I try to know facts from the beginning of the client's life to the present time, even if my client is an older person. I want to be able to visualize how this person came to be, in which family, how were their first years of life, the beginning of their adult life until today.

It is believed that a person's personality structure is largely formed before the age of seven. Early childhood determines much of the common anxieties within the personality, as well as the defenses developed to deal with these anxieties - it is these same defenses that, in many cases, will constitute the adult symptoms. Therefore, more than labeling the client with a diagnostic picture, we should be able to answer, at the end of this anamnesis, what were this person's childhood anxieties, how he/she survived and how he/she self-medicated in order to deal with his problems.

1 – Family constellation:
* Name and age of parents and children and birth order of siblings.

2- Parents' History:
* Did your parents marry for love?
* How did they decide to have children?
* Were the children planned?
* Was your pregnancy expected?
* Did your parents expect it to be a boy or a girl?
* What do you know about your pregnancy?

3 – Birth:
* What do you know about your birth?
* Have you been breastfed? How was breastfeeding? Did you sleep well?

4 – Early childhood:
* What do you remember from your early childhood?
* How was your parents' relationship?
* Who was the angriest?
* How did your parents set boundaries?
* Who really liked being with you?
* Do you remember your brothers back then?
* Who did you get along with best? Did you have many friends?

5 – School:
* When did you start going to school?
* How was it?
* Were you a good student? Did you have friends?

6 – Adolescence:
* When was your first period?
* What was it like to become "young woman/man?
* Did you have friends at this time?
* Did you think you were beautiful? Did you have a boyfriend or a girlfriend?

7 – Sexuality:
* At what age did you start having sex?
* Was it good or was it bad?
* Who were the most important boyfriends or girlfriends?
* How long did it last and why did it end?

FIGURE 1 - ANAMNESIS SCRIPT

After these verbal interviews I perform a Social Atom. I tell my client that in the third interview we will use Psychodrama so that he/she knows the way I work. (see figure 4 pg. 67).

Throughout this process, I tend to confirm my patient's dramatic ability by showing him/her that his ability to perform these role reversals is enough for us to use psychodrama with them.

Many patients have shown difficulties since this time; some talk to me and not to the pillow; others speak of the counter-role, but not with it. I will point out these subtleties to the patient. I tell them to speak in the first person singular, looking at them, talking to them, etc.

I believe this cautious introduction to psychodrama favors more complex dramatizations in the future. Finally, I do a feedback interview and the contract. Below I transcribe (Figure 3) a contract written by me, but I suggest that each therapist write their own. Writing our own rules is a great way to clarify what we think.

A - TIME
• The Therapy Schedule , will be pre-fixed between therapist and patient. If the patient needs to unmark, he will bear the "time burden". If the therapist needs to clear, he will not charge the fee.

B-SCHEDULE REPLACEMENT-
• Whenever the patient needs to cancel a time, he must call 24 hours in advance. The therapist will then designate another time within that week. If the client can come this new time I can replace it, otherwise he/she will miss the session in question. It must be clear that the new schedule will be assigned by the therapist according to his possibilities.
• Whenever the therapist needs to substitute a schedule, they should contact the patient and be aware of their availability. If the patient cannot accept any of the times the therapist offers, the therapist will not charge for the unbooked time.

B-HOLIDAYS
• For two months a year, January and July, the patient will have unpaid vacations, if he wants to take them, otherwise he/she will arrange vacation times with the therapist.
• If the client takes a vacation, or travels outside of this period, he/she will pay the time normally.
• If the therapist travels outside of this period, he/she will not charge fees.

C-REMUNERATION
• The remuneration of the sessions will depend on an agreement established between the therapist and the client.
• Increase in fees will normally be governed by the country's inflation system, and will depend on an agreement between Therapist and Patient.
• Fees will be charged every fortnight or at the end of the month until, at the latest, the 5th of the month due. After this period, the amount paid will be increased by monthly inflation, and/or, it will depend on the agreement with the therapist.

FIG.3: THERAPEUTIC EMPLOYMENT CONTRACT FOR BIPERSONAL PSYCHODRAMATIC PSYCHOTHERAPY

Figure 4 summarizes the basic framing of the therapeutic work in bipersonal format:

- Running time - 50-60 minutes

- Frequency of dramatization – role play is not compulsory, but frequent.

- Weekly frequency - once or twice a week

- Complementary roles - are signaled by pillows or objects in the room

- Action of complementary roles = the patient plays the roles with the pillows and inverts with them.

- Role of the therapist: the therapist is extremely active in the role playing with pillows ,toys and objects in the room , and basically performs two verbal actions that keep the patient warmed up:
- A. Uses the interview technique, as a "voice from beyond", a playful voice and accomplice of all roles, which interviews and is friendly with all the roles that the client presents.
- B. When the client returns to his/HER own role, the therapist lends his/her voice and physical strength to the pillow (or toy, or object) referring to it in the 3rd person singular, and summarizing the conflicting context for the client. For example: look X, look at what your father said and look at the position of his arms, what do you think?
- C. The therapist rarely or briefly acts with the client
- All other classical psychodrama techniques are used in the same way as role playing.

FIGURE 4 - BASIC FRAMING

2-Assist the client – he/she and not the therapist - to choose, focus and deepen a theme and decide whether it is better to use an open scene psychodrama or an internal psychodrama.

Many therapists, young or not, believe it is their job to decide which scene to dramatize. They then listen to the patient's initial speech with attention directed at "picking up" a scene that lends itself to a session beginning, as if they were using a fishing rod. Needless to say, our patients are very smart fish, ruled by their fears and defenses against change. They learned, during their dysfunctional childhood life, a victimized passivity, were submitted to authoritarian parents. Prevented from reacting and fighting their aggression, they had to hide their real desires, they disguised their hates and angers, in short, they are masters of showing a lethargic and powerless posture in the face of reality and their own life. It seems that something must change, but they don't feel capable of making this change.

In many verbal therapies, when mainly interpretation is used, the key to the symbolic puzzle seems to be in the hands of the therapist. The patient is the patient - they wait for the therapist to do their job and this only reinforces their learned fragility and impotence.

Dalmiro Bustos had a picture frame in his office, with the following sentence: "what was said about me that I didn't find out by myself doesn't serve me". I think the great advantage of dramatization is that it favors the active and responsible research of the patient in relation to their problem. All clients have a healthy and combative part and I make this known to them since the beginning of our meetings. I make no alliance with the lethargic and helpless part of them. I always ask them what they want to work on in that particular session and have them act out the situations they choose to work on. They are active researchers, like me and deciphering their material, their emotions, decisions, is our joint task and often more their task than mine. (Figure 5) shows some tips to help the patient choose a topic and commit to it.

My clients usually choose their themes and take responsibility for them and, as soon as they do it, I decide which psychodramatic resource I will use[33]. This is my share of responsibility: knowing and realizing when to administer the techniques.

---

33 For a better description of the techniques, see *Bipersonal psychodrama:* its techniques, therapies, and clients (Cukier, 1993).

At the beginning of the session, after the initial greetings, listen to the client for about 10 minutes and then ask them through one of these questions:
- What do you want to work on today?Among these issues you described, which one is of interest to you to work more deeply today? (I usually get up and solve each of the problems with a cushion. What help do you expect from me in this question you described?
- Sometimes the client responds that he/she doesn't want to work on anything, just share what happened. I don't see any problem with sharing questions, as long as it's not customary conduct in every session.

• Other times the customer says he doesn't know what to choose. Then I usually ask you if you want help choosing a topic. This is a paradoxical offer, as as soon as the client accepts it (and 99% of my clients accept it) I propose one of the tasks below, aiming only to make them active in this search.
- Walk around the room, stretch, think about the last few weeks and separate, with the help of cushions, the difficult situations or scenes you went through.
- Look at the masks (I have a panel of them on my wall) which one attracts you today? Which one would you like to try a little bit)
- Flip through this photo book (Coutinho and Caram, 2000), choose one or two and read the text that is written on the back. Does it remind you of something in your life?
- Think about the relationship that currently bothers you the most, bring this person here to therapy (choose a pillow to play his/her role). So I start doing an "interview with the enemy" trying to find out what he thinks my patient needs to work on himself.

• As for those clients who chronically say they just want to talk, I usually explain to them at length what it means to "do therapy". Basically, I try to differentiate the relief obtained by discharging the conflicts through speech – the "toilet effect of the therapy " – from the elaboration of the conflicts.
- This last task is complex and involves more than just talking about life; it is necessary to understand old repetitions, expand the range of possible responses and understand our emotional susceptibility. That's why it's important to choose a topic and go deeper into it, research it, not just talk about it.

FIGURE 5 - CHOOSING A THEME

I mostly use psychodrama with an open scene (CUKIER, 1998, p. 67-72) unless the client is unable to move around or is exploring a topic that he/she is ashamed of or is someone who hates to dramatize. As for internal psychodrama, I use it in three situations:

1- When the patient has nonspecific complaints (body pain, generalized anguish, etc.)

2- When the investigated themes cause embarrassment or shame to the patient.

3- When the patient has a "hystericoform" personality, looking more interested in impressing me and controlling than exploring their own themes.

3. Warming up and warming up maintenance in open scene psychodrama and in internal psychodrama

In bipersonal psychodrama, despite the short session time, we cannot skip the warm-up. It is very important for us to achieve the expected results. However, there is little consensus and almost no discussion about the time we should spend in each of its stages (warm-up, role-play, and sharing), both in bipersonal and group therapy. Sometimes, with hardly any warm-up, we see colleagues start a drama action. At other times, we observe such prolonged warm-ups that there is almost no time for the dramatization.

This indefiniteness in my opinion, comes from Moreno himself. He, despite mentioning several times in his work the importance of what he calls the warm-up, does not describe in depth any of these procedures. Some people who were in Beacon (Moreno's Theater) surprised us when they told us that the sessions started a little "dry", without much previous preparation, that is, without much premeditated unspecific warm-up.

I think that the non-specific warm-up in a 50-minute individual session should take, more or less, the initial 5 to 10 minutes of the session. The role play, including the specific warm-up, takes about 25 to 30 minutes, leaving 10 to 15 minutes for the sharing portion. These are not absolute times, obviously, but they serve as a guideline so that the session does not go without a warm-up, nor does it run out of it.

Finally, we need to seriously consider the fact that no one can disconnect from the random stresses of everyday life (traffic, children, etc.) and connect to an emotional issue or even play a role if not warmed up. And the therapist him/herself cannot do his/her job and keep the client warm if he/she is not warmed up him/herself. Moreno said that the "director's spontaneity is what warms the patient", so the therapist him/herself needs to find a way to warm up and put him/herself in a half playful, half magical, half mysterious state for the psychodrama to happen.

I find this aspect one of the most difficult to achieve as a therapist, because we need to be very confident in the technique and confident in our performance so as not to be afraid of ridicule and, in fact, invite our clients to do what they believe to be impossible.

The best way to achieve this state is to dive into the scene that is brought to us through an interview that seeks to detail the space where it takes place and the description of the characters who participate in it. It is in the details that the emotional memory is hidden, as in the case of the vase, forgotten at the end of the shelf, which the client got at the age of 15 from her father and where she currently deposits the tears of her father's grief.

Warming up

My golden rule for warming up is to ask for details until I myself, the therapist, locate myself in that kitchen, or backyard; I have to be able to see the room, look out the window, realize that I am short next to my tall, strong father, etc. We need to look for important details without getting lost in the superfluous.

The first scene is the one that needs the most details, because it takes place at the beginning of the session and everyone, therapist and client, is literally cold and needs to warm up a lot. In the other scenes, or confrontations, not so many particularities will be necessary, but the active presence of a therapist who maintains the warm-up already achieved is necessary. This is done through verbalizations that summarize the facts, in general, in the third person singular.

Figure 6 summarizes this procedure and also the specific warm-up for internal psychodrama, if this is the chosen form of work. In this case, the specific warm-up will involve some procedure that facilitates introspection and helps the patient to focus on him/herself. Any task that involves paying attention to one´s breathing helps. I usually use one that suggests the patient to breathe, marking different times for inspiration and expiration. It is only necessary to take special care not to exaggerate this relaxation to the point that the client falls asleep and does not perform the work, as this is not our objective.

1- **Working with the initial scene: connecting transferential scenes and how to articulate time - present, past, and future - in the dramatization.**

After the patient chooses what he/she wants to work on, the therapist must decide what kind of role play to do. In principle, all drama is exploratory, that is to say, we do not know what exactly it will result in.

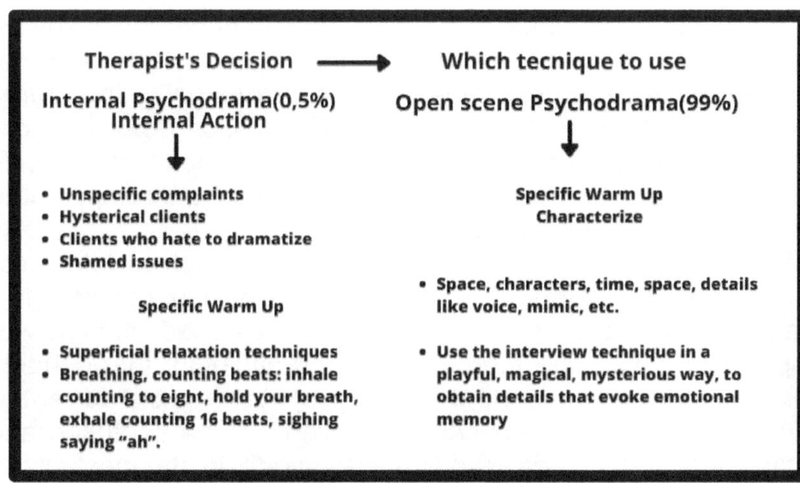

FIGURE 6 - WARMING UP

Therefore, the therapist's first attitude must be very neutral and probing. I suggest starting the specific warm-up by asking the client details about the physical space and the characters that interact in the scene. Usually, by the time the therapist manages to visualize the site and the people interacting there, the patient will be warm enough.

After setting the scene, we ask the client to take his/her own role and do what he/she did before followed by a soliloquy. We can interview him/her during the soliloquy. Then we ask him/her to take the place of each of the characters and we also ask for an action, followed by the soliloquy and our interview. After this phase, we place the patient in a mirror and ask him/her: "What help do you need here?". It is the patient's response that will tell us how to continue this dramatization. Figure 7 outlines this procedure.

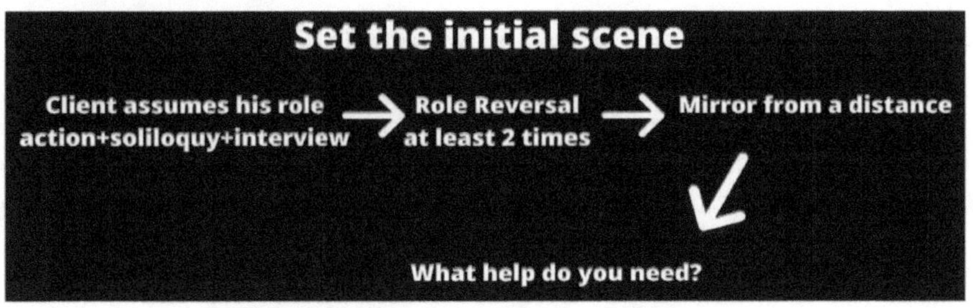

FIGURE 7- SET THE INITIAL SCENE

If the client responds that he/she needs to understand why he/she acts in a certain way, the therapist should help him/her to look for the matrix of the behavior he/she repeats. This implies using the regressive scene technique to research the functionality of such repetitive action in the past. If, however, the client needs to learn to dialogue or train different roles, the work proposal will unfold in the present through role play, confrontations, dialogues, etc.

It is also possible that the client's need involves future scenes that have not yet occurred but are already causing conflicts in their imagination. In this case, several resources can be used, such as working in an open scene with the feared or desired situation, the technique of sculpture, etc. It is very important to always go back to the current scene where the drama started, otherwise the client will be confused and not understand what that understanding was worth in the past or future. Figure 8 summarizes this articulation of past, present and future in dramatization.

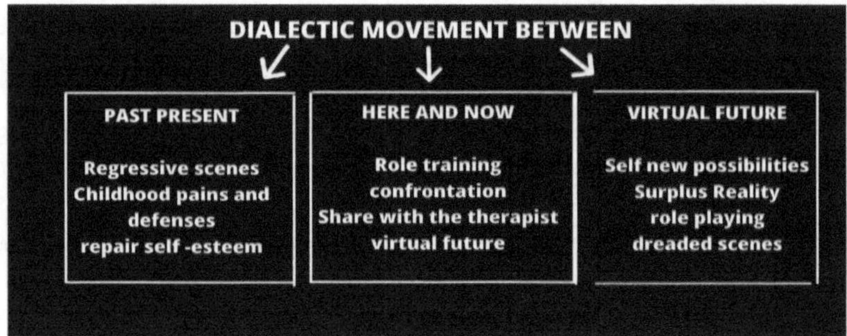

FIGURE 8 - TIME IN DRAMATIZATION

2- Decide which technique, among the existing ones, to use.

Figure 9 shows the systematization I made of the techniques I use in my book *"Bipersonal Psychodrama"* (CUKIER, 1993). I believe there are as many techniques as there are therapists and I always suggest to my students that one day they should list and try to organize the techniq

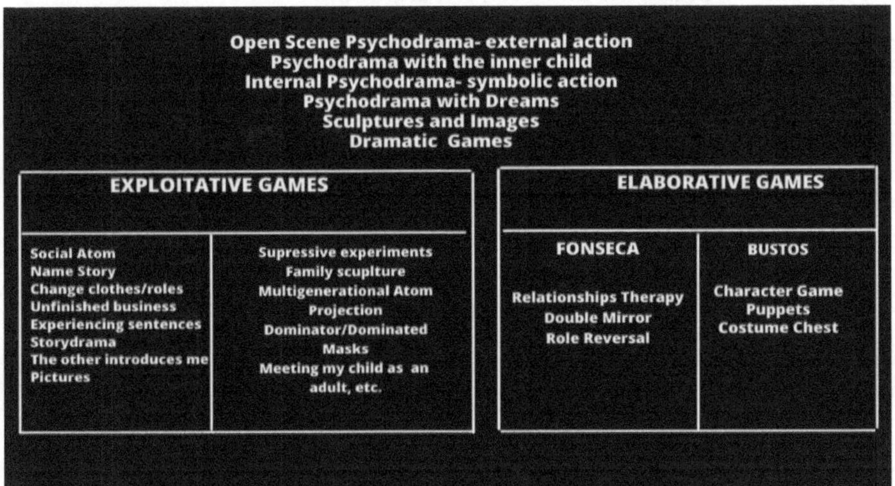

FIGURE 9 - LIST OF TECHNIQUES

6. PSYCHODRAMA WITH REGRESSIVE SCENES

Among the various resources (Pitzele, P., 1992)[1] that psychodrama offers us to work with, psychodrama with Regressive Scenes is in my opinion the one that most deeply explores the problems related to self-esteem and narcissism. This type of psychodrama is commonly called 'psychoanalytical', 'intrapsychic', or 'Bustos's psychodrama'[2]. Some of us believe that it is an important contribution to the Morenian body of work, while others think that it distorts his purpose; in short, I believe that we still have not named or even adequately explored what type of psychodrama this is and how it operates.

When working with a regressive scene, the client normally comes to the session with some current complaint, relational or not, which he/she cannot really deal with. The psychodramatist, after doing some type of

---

[1] Peter Pitzele, American psychodramatist, summarizes in a simple way three types of psychodramatic methods: 1- Interpersonal Psychodrama, which investigates an individual's past, present, and future interpersonal relationships; 2- Surrealistic Psychodrama, which investigates dreams, metaphors, fantasies - anything that escapes formal logic and is in the dominion of what Moreno called 'Supplementary Reality'; 3- Intrapsychic Psychodrama, which attempts to discriminate roles, interior voices, parts and characters which inhabit a person's interior world.

[2] Actually, Bustos uses various techniques; not only this one.

warm-up, suggests setting up this present situation.

After this, and according to indicators (Bustos,*1985:* 42-43)[3] which arise, he/she goes along a transferential chain (Perazzo,1987) of scene associations until reaching a certain scene which we could call nuclear or matrix. (Figure 3.1)

CLIENT ARRIVES WITH SEVERAL SCENES WITH NEGATIVE SELF-ESTEEM	→	TRANSFERENTIAL CHAIN SEVERAL SCENES IN THE PAST WITH NEGATIVE SELF-ESTEEM	→	NUCLEAR SCENE NEGATIVE SELF-ESTEEM

FIGURE 3.1. SESSION USING REGRESSIVE SCENES

This nuclear scene is one of the *locus* (Bustos, 1994)[4] of the client's difficulties; it is the relationship for which the client structured a type of defensive response that turned out to be useful for the occasion. However, because of its crystallization, it ended up creating the present difficulties.

Here are some nuclear scene's common denominators when dramatized:

- Normally they occur very *early* in life - before eight years of age.

- The content of the *related drama* is of a child being neglected or punished by some significant adult, or even a child who sees some adult showing disrespect in an abusive way towards other people in his/her social atom.

- The child normally submits him/herself, with anger, shame, and impotence to the adult because he/she is fragile and does not have

---

[3] Bustos talks about three indicators: mental - thoughts, visual images, everything which appears in symbolic form; the emotional indicator - intermediary productions between the body and the mind which appear in the form of anguish or varied emotions; and finally, the bodily indicator which corresponds to varied sensations, such as areas of greater bodily oppression or constriction, comfort and areas of well-being, etc.

[4] Bustos (1994) uses the Morenian concepts of *Locus, Status Nascendi* and *Matrix,* as a theoretical structure that guides therapeutic work. First, we research *What* the client needs to work on; after what the *Locus* of the problem is - the place, the special combination of family and social conditions that surrounded the client when the problem arose. Following this, we search for the *Status Nascendi* - the temporal dimension, the moment in which the facts took place. Finally, we try to identify the *Matrix* - the client's possible response and its function in these circumstances. The psychodramatic therapist aims at the Re-matrixation - to help the client to find a new response to the old circumstances.

any way of reacting. The dramatization, besides exposing this resentful submission, reveals a psychic action by the child, who looks to rescue his/her dignity and self-esteem in some way. Many times, it is a type of confrontation and force pact, a type of promise for the future. It aims at reassuring the child that when he/she grows up, nobody will ever do that to him/her again or to the people that he/she loves. Other times, the psychic action is of a schizoid type, and consists of removing the feeling (shame, anger, humiliation) as if internally the decision were: "Nothing or nobody is ever going to reach me again." The important thing is that there is some kind of psychic activity that tries to avoid the previous humiliating situation.

Behind the current drama that the client brings to our office there is an internal one, the one of the child who he/she was one day, and who tries to rescue the wounded self-esteem and dignity. Once this wounded child is recognized, the therapeutic process consists of understanding his/her pain and the promises that he/she made to himself when he/she was growing up.

A client, for example, presented herself as someone extremely aggressive, the kind who intimidates and fights with everyone and only later realizes what she did. Among the important facts from her childhood was the strong presence of an older sister, who had fits of rage and physically attacked everybody in the house. This woman grew up comforted by the promise of one day being as strong as, or stronger than, her sister, so that nobody would ever terrorize her again. Another client of mine is in an apparently opposite situation, completely apathetic, who decided to never take any risks and always be the 'good guy' with everyone. He in fact did not feel anything; his motto was: "If I am already dead, nobody can kill me anymore" [sic]. As a child, an extremely violent alcoholic father beat him and his mother.

Returning to the childhood scene evidently did not change either the sister or the father of these people, but helped them understand their own pain. It also helped them renegotiate the promises they had made in the past with themselves and be able to cope with the situation differently.

In therapy, we try for a meeting with this child within to bring about a type of negotiation and re-decision process as the child's concrete thoughts make him/her imagine very radical solutions that are not always valid throughout life.

The client's adult side needs to understand this child within, negotiate with it and obtain other alternatives that will not endanger happiness in his/her present life. Fig. 3.3 shows this process.

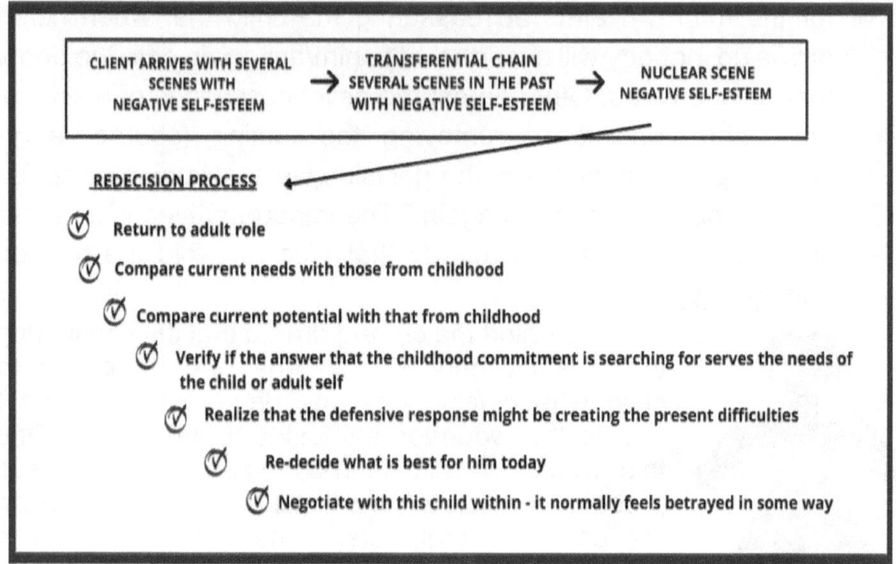

Fig. 3.3. Diagram for working with the nuclear scene

One of the therapeutic factors of psychodrama with regressive scenes, from my point of view, is that it promotes the repairing of old damage, which I call 'Self-esteem Maintenance System or Narcissistic System of the client'. As I explained before, this consists of a type of self-evaluating center or, using Morenian terms, a permanent social and self-metric center which we have in our psychism and informs us every minute what our value is for the other and for ourselves. Restructuring and detailing we would have:

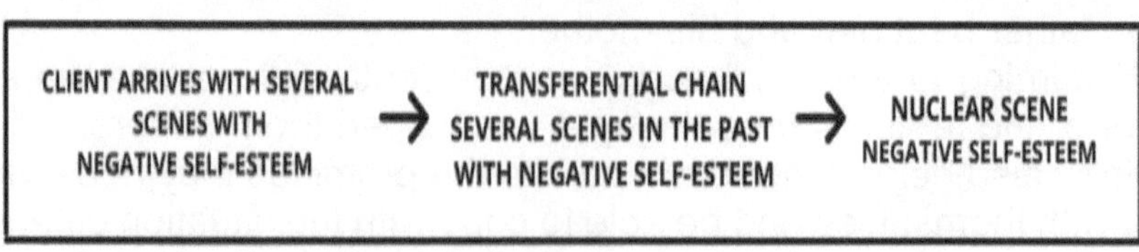

FIG. 3.4. REGRESSIVE SCENE AND NARCISSISM

With his/her complaint, the client brings us a situation in which he/she is not feeling well (vulnerable self-esteem). Following along this transferential course by way of free-scene associations, we will find various other scenes from his/her life in which he/she also felt fragile and will end up, most of the time, with some childhood scene (nuclear scene) in which his/her relational difficulties were immense.

Dramatizing this nuclear scene and researching the *locus*, *status nascendi* and *matrix* of his/her current difficulties and pain, we will find the 'narcissistic wounds' (Kohut, 1984) of the client's child within and understand the defensive techniques that he/she needed to create to balance his/her narcissism and be able to grow.

Most of the time, our client's current problems are the result of the crystallization of these childhood defenses. The therapy aims at releasing the adult's spontaneity (Moreno, 1992: 159)[5] and helping him/her to substitute the old 'remedies' for others that are more efficient and adapted to his current narcissism. For example, certain facts which deeply bothered him/her at a time in which he/she was functioning according to the logic of exclusion might not bother him so much anymore in the present. Perhaps he does not need such a thick suit of armor to defend him/herself now.

Conclusion

In our circles it is very often believed that psychodrama's central therapeutic strategy is summed up in the final analysis by Moreno's relational proposal – that psychodrama heals through the 'therapeutic encounter'. This type of belief presupposes a rematrixation of the subject's relational capacity, starting almost exclusively from the therapeutic bond and the diverse group bonds that the clients create between themselves.

Personally, I have proven psychodrama's efficiency with regressive scenes in the treatment of various disturbances, especially when narcissistic issues are involved. I believe that an ideal therapeutic posture must dialectically contain the intrapsychic technique (in which the dynamic of narcissism that I discussed in this book is included) and the inter-relational (sociometry and socio-dynamic are also included here).

I think it misleading to call psychodrama with regressive scenes psychoanalytical, as it never stops being a relational psychotherapy. It is

---

[5] For Moreno, spontaneity meant: "the driving force of the individual in the direction of the appropriate response to a new situation, or a new response to an already known situation."

not interpretive; it does not work producing transference neurosis; and it does not operate through resistance analysis.

It is a post-Morenian and post-psychoanalytical psychodrama, which takes extremely important parts from both theories. However, it maintains – and therefore deserves the name of psychodrama – not only the technique, but Moreno's philosophical existential postulates and conception of man.

7. Ending dramatization and how to manage the end of the session when time runs out in the middle of the action

A dramatization with the regressive scene is exhausted only when the client:

• Relives the pain of the childhood scene.
• Can understand how they managed to survive.
• Understands current problems caused by their child's defenses.
• Trains new adult and appropriate forms of action, modifying their current conduct.

Obviously, a 50–60-minute session is not enough time to fit in all these aspects. There were cases in which I spent about three months working on the same scene until I understood all the connections. Remember that this work represents the center of the hurricane, it is the most important bullet in our trigger, and we should nor burn it in vain by going too fast.

There are many ways to end a session in the middle of this work, leaving certain hooks to warm up the patient and continue into the next week. These are strategic tasks, according to the moment of the regressive scene where the session time has run out, which must be done at home:

• Bring a written text to the next session with details about what happened in this scene and, if you have a photo of yourself from this time, bring it too.
• Write a letter to yourself as a child. Make sure you write it in children's language, as a child under 8 years old is going to read it.
• Make a collage or find a photo on the Internet of the character who carries his child defense.
• Take a picture of this scene on an imaginary Polaroid and we will continue with it next week.

• Write a letter to the characters in this scene—father, mother, brother, etc. What would you say to them today about what happened in the children's scene?

• Imagine if the greatest lawyer in the world could take the defense of this child, what would his/her argument be?

• What would the child you once were ask you today if they could?

Sometimes the client does not want to continue the work the next week, because he/she has something more urgent to work on, or because he/she does not feel ready to go into the old anguish. The task is then postponed until he/she can take it up again, and do not worry, because that will happen sooner or later. Other times the client does not do the task at home, forgets about it or does not want to do it. We can help him/her go through it during the session or let him/her bring it up next time. It is always good to discuss why the task has not been done, as it is an agreement with the therapist that has been made and broken. We must always know why and consider what happened.

I wanted to conclude this text by telling therapists with difficulty in dramatizing to try to share their doubts with a supervisor who dramatizes and is supportive of the initial doubts. The ability to be a psychodrama director gradually forms, like a sculpture molded into the director's own emotional skin.

I have never met anyone who was not afraid to direct at the beginning, who has never gotten lost in the middle of scenes, who has never felt embarrassed about showing their doubts to the supervisor. It is up to us, supervisors, to receive these initial ambiguities with respect, affection and understanding, so that the students themselves can contain them and do not feel any phobias about the task.

REFERENCES

BUSTOS, M. D. (1994) **Wings and Roots** - in Psicodrama since Moreno - by Paul Holmes and Marcia Karp and Michael Watson- Routledge.- pp 63-77.
COUTINHO, B.; CARAN, C. Caution: if you continue on this path… *In*: Images, reflections, and exercises for self-knowledge. Belo Horizonte, Minas Gerais: Crescer, 2000.
CUKIER, Rosa. Bipersonal Psychodrama: Its Techniques, Therapists, and Clients"?. Lulu.com

__________. Emotional Survival: Childhood Pain Relived in the Drama of Adult Life?, Lulu.com

MORENO, Jacob Levy. Who shall survive? Fundamentals of sociometry, group psychotherapy and sociodrama. Goiânia: Dimensão, 1992.

KOHUT, H. (2000). **Analysis of the Self: Systematic Approach to Treatment of Narcissistic Personality Disorders**; International Universities Press

MORENO, J.L (1978)- **Who Shall Survive? Foundations of Sociometry, Group Psychotherapy and Sociodrama.** Beacon House Inc., New York.

PERAZZO, S. (1987) Percurso Transferencial e Reparação , Revista Temas, ano XVII, nº 32-33.

PITZELE, P. (1990) – **Adolescents: intrapsiquic psychodrama-** in Psychodrama: Inspiration and Technique Routledge, London.

THE PSYCHOSOCIAL DRAMA OF ENVY: THROW THE FIRST STONE IF YOU DARE [34]

Introduction

I have never been able to cope with the emotional experience of envy[35]. Neither my own, horribly embittered inside my thoughts, nor the others', wisely denied and exteriorized with touches of resentment and rejection.

After reading a vast amount of literature over the last few years, I perceived that, of all human life experiences, envy is the least studied and about which the least was written, especially in psychology. Only human sexuality had been repressed so much in other times.

Some authors say that there is no dignity in such a feeling. Even extreme rage and hatred may be explained by any noble reason, but envy always represents an obscure feeling, without legal justification, mean and isolated, futile, hidden - as it best suits bandits, thieves and assassins, the scum of the human race.

And, however, throw the first stone if you have never felt it! If you have never wished someone evil based on an attribute you admired, if you have never avoided situations in which you had to confront people exhibiting qualities that you lack, and if you have never sided with someone just to not favor those who possessed aspects you coveted, etc. "Practically everything that brings happiness stimulates envy", said Aristoteles.

And perhaps you may also have never thought that without envy, and the consequent capacity of always comparing and watching

34 Article published in the **Brazilian Psychodrama Journal,** v. 19, n. 1, p. 13-35, 2011.
35 For Antonio Damasio, a sentiment is a mental representation, a perception of the state of the body, whereas emotion is a reaction to a stimulus and a behavior associated (for example, a facial expression). Therefore, a sentiment is the recognition of an event that is occurring, while emotion is the visible effect of the same. Emotions are corporal things, whereas sentiments are mental things. Emotions are an automatic response. They do not require any thinking. They are the fundamental mechanism for the regulation of life. Emotions precede sentiments and are the basis for them. I think that envy is a set of sentiment/emotion, that is why I decided to adopt the term emotional experience in this text, because it is more inclusive. So, the feeling is the recognition that an event is taking place, whereas emotions are bodily things.

ourselves mutually, we would not have the development of social systems to which we all belong. Consider also how it lies sovereign, like a drab eminence, behind social and economic policies and almost all revolutionary movements of the history of mankind.

According to Helmut Schoeck (1987), there are crimes caused by envy, policies based on envy, institutions meant to regulate envy and numerous reasons to avoid being envied by others.

Molded in a feeling of injustice by differences (whatever they might be: financial, aesthetic, philosophical) and in the idea that everyone should be equally favored, many policies of expropriation were conducted. From the XVIII century, with the emblematic motto of the French revolution - "equality, fraternity and freedom" - until the socialist revolutions (XIX and XX centuries), this philosophy of equality is proclaimed, an opium for the feeling of envy, which gains demagogic strength in this apparently fair indignation.

According to de La Mora (1987) envy is the biggest unspoken human taboo; everyone feels it, but few admit it, which makes its study hard and indirect. Curiously, however, when honorably vesting this ideological carcass of equality, it becomes the bastion of human justice. The same author concludes his great book "*Equalitarian Envy*" arguing for the healthy necessity of the difference, and for the absurdity of one's imagining that equality may be conquered by coercion or demagogy.

Just out of curiosity, and already approaching psychology and psychodrama, we know that envy is a feeling apprehended in cluster one and massively externalized in cluster three (BUSTOS, 1994, p. 362), cluster of symmetrical, fraternal and amorous roles, with the dynamics of cooperation, competition and rivalry. We do not usually envy kings and queens and their fortunes accumulated without manual work, but we may envy our next-door neighbor, because he/she bought a brand new car. Cain and Abel's story appears to be the right metaphor to illustrate this sentiment.

Well, we are all different. And we have to learn how to cope with these differences. Is it ever possible? How can we learn to deal with the differences? How can we better live with the primordial injustice of human existence? What should I do when I feel envious? How to cope with other people's envy? Have I really provoked their envy? Can someone who envies me, cause me any harm, the famous "evil eye"? These are the questions that make me research this theme. That is why I also propose the psychosocial drama[36] of envy, in the hopes that we do not remain

---

36 I have chosen to use the term psycho sociodrama for I believe that the theme of envy is at the same time collective and individual. Moreno (1975, p. 383-5) says that

silent over shameful themes, but, on the contrary, respectfully united follow this arid path.

1.   Concept

"The number of those who envy us confirms our capabilities".
<u>Oscar Wilde</u>

The word envy comes from the Latin *in-videre*, which means "not see", or "see biasedly". Envy manifests itself popularly through "greedy eyes", the "evil eye" - the devil's eye. To be seen seems to be essential to the envy theme, either to those who are envied (they are seen) or those who envy (they see). This psychological phenomenon presupposes a social context: the coexistence of two people.

Numerous definitions of this feeling range according to the aspect of the phenomenon we want to tackle:

- Envy is a kind of psychological pain felt when comparing ourselves to other people, we conclude that our value, self-esteem and our respect are diminished.
- Envy is a painful observation of what we are lacking.
- We feel envy when another person has characteristics that are superior to ours.
- Envy is a type of admiration and love for something we lack.
- *Schadenfreude* is a German word also used in other languages to designate the feeling of joy or pleasure for the suffering or misfortune of others.
- Envy is a feeling that invades us when we observe other people's success.

In all languages - from the primitive ones to the Hindu-European, Arabic, Japanese, Chinese - there is a term that designates an envious person. The primitive polygamous societies already had policies to deal with envy, especially related to the distribution of affection and goods

---

Psychodrama refers to "private" problems, but as soon as individuals are treated as collective representatives of the roles of the community and of the relations of roles, not taking into account their private roles and their relations of private roles, the psychodrama converts into a "socio psychodrama" or, more briefly into a sociodrama.

equally among wives and descendents. A lot of conflicts took place due to inequalities and a lot of superstitions were created to magically obtain the desired benefits. (SCHOECK, 1987).

Envy is therefore a universal phenomenon, and literature, religion and philosophy are full of studies and metaphors on this subject. Look at the following:

- *"Because he possesses herbs and grains...he is envied by the Philistines". (***Bible.*** Gn 26, 14-15).*
- *"Envy sees only the bridge, not the span that covers it"; "For envious eyes, a mosquito becomes an elephant"; Envy sees the ship quite well, but not the hole in its hull, etc. (Russian literature).*
- *"Fear Allah and do not envy his power"." Envy devours faith like fire devours wood". (*Islamic literature).
- *"Envy is the pain caused by the good fortune of others"* (ARISTOTLE. **Rhetoric**: book II. p. 10).
- *"Envy wishes to destroy the good fortune of others".* (KANT, Immanuel. **Metaphysics of Moral**. p. 459).
- *"Envy is the passion that sees malign displeasure in the superiority of those who have the capacity to deserve the superiority they possess".* (SMITH, Adam. **The Theory of Moral Sentiments**. p. 244, 1759).

However, to conceptualize this feeling is not an easy task; one can confuse it with the complex feeling of jealousy and this discrimination must be made. Another difficulty emerges from the possible gradations of this feeling. It is then that we hear about good envy, very close to admiration and easy to be admitted, in opposition to "bad envy", which is really similar to the German word *Schadenfreude*, consisting of a real torment before the good fortune of the others and an extreme pleasure in their misfortune.

2.   Envy & Jealousy

«Jealousy fears losing its possessions; envy suffers watching the other having what it wants for itself".

It is not always easy to separate envy from jealousy. Both feelings presuppose social interactions, comparisons among individuals and are extremely harmful for the relationships. Envy generally refers to a dual relationship, in which the subject misses something the other possesses and wishes he/she would not have it, whereas jealousy has to do with triangular relationships and basically consists of the fear of losing a relationship for another person. Envy prefers to destroy while jealousy aims to control.

A flaw can be found in both feelings. In jealousy, the flaw refers to the fear of losing something or someone who is already "yours" to somebody else; the flaw in envy refers to something that you don't have, but the other person does. Both feelings are externalized very similarly: they are partly denied, but appear indirectly under the fear of losing, rage, cheating, insecurity, inferiority, vengeance, paranoia, among others.

Foster (1972, p. 167) suggests that envy provokes jealousy as a counter-reaction, as if they were complementary. For instance, if someone feels that his beautiful wife is being coveted, he becomes jealous, fearing losing her. The same happens to any object or attribute that is wanted: he/she who has something does not want to lose it, and he/she who does not possess something wants to get it, at least, does not want the other to have it.

3.　　　Good Envy & Bad Envy

Maybe to minimize the impact of such a shameful feeling, or to dialectically avoid the false polarities between good and bad, some authors argue that envy has at least one positive factor, since it can be the fuel or an extra motivation to reach success or acquire attributes leading to happiness.

For Jung (1991) analytical psychology, no matter what trace of character or attitude exists in the conscious and dominating mind, its opposite equally reigns in the unconscious. The repressed content in the unconscious must become conscious to produce a tension of the opposites, and thus make the personality flexible and enrich it. Says the author:

"All this process is called "transcendent function". It is at the same time a process and a method. The production of unconscious compensations is a spontaneous process, whereas the conscious realization is a method. The function is called "transcendent" because it favors the passage of psychic constitution to the other, through the mutual confrontation of the opposites (JUNG, 1991, p. 15)".

Byington (2002, p. 21-2) talks about the creative potential of envy, which would be only one of the structuring functions of the Psyche, being able to act creatively and provide the healthy development of the personality or, on the contrary, become fixed and begin to act in the Shade[37]·, in an inadequate, repetitive and destructive way.

In an article about the work of Gonzalo Fernández de La Mora (1987), "Equalitarian Envy", the author Eduardo O. C. Chaves (1991) shows that, in view of the possibility of the others becoming happier than us, it is possible to assume one of the three attitudes:

a) Emulation: the desire to be like the others, act like them, and possess the things they possess.

b) Resignation: to accept our (real or supposed) inferiority.

c) Envy: to wish the others would lose what they have and wish it were ours.

The attitude of emulation is positive; it triggers progress and human development. The more it stimulates competition, the better. Fernández de La Mora says: "Do what you have to do and do it better than anyone else" − referring to sports in general, which would not have progressed had people not tried to improve it.

The attitude of resignation may have negative and positive aspects. It is negative because as the subject resigns, he/she fails to contribute to progress and human development, leading to stagnation. It does not promote involution, though.

The attitude of envy, however, is just negative because it leads to involution. The envious individual wishes misfortune and misery to those he/she envies; he/she wants to see those superior to him/her be reduced to his/her level.

Briefly, I think that it is possible to use envy as a catalyst of energy toward envied objects, more or less like a plan of life or ambition. This would be the good envy, the emulation that causes no harm to anyone, neither to those who try it nor to those serving as its target. To admit it would do good to the self in the sense that Kohut meant to affirm: "we are pushed by our ambitions and led by our ideals".

---

37 For Jung, the shadow is the center of the personal unconscious, the nucleus of the material repressed by the conscience. The shadow includes those tendencies, desires, memories, and experiences that are rejected by the individual as incompatible with the persona, and contrary to social standards and ideals. The shadow represents what we consider inferior in our personality and what we neglect and never developed in ourselves. In dreams, the shadow often appears as an animal, a dwarf, a vagabond, or any other figure of lower category.

However, the focus of my paper today is not this benign envy, but the other one that makes you suffer by the impact of observing other people's attributes that point to our own inferiority and ends up in a personal impotence and desire to destroy the other. My focus is the so-called *"Green Envy"*, a term coined by Shakespeare in Othello, referring to jealousy - probably an allusion to the hepatic bile, a viscous digestive yellowish-green secretion produced by the liver and as bitter as this sentiment.

4.   Origins of Envy

"When one of my friends is successful, something dies inside me".
Gore Vidal

Why are some people more envious than others? Is envy inborn or is it learned? The origins of envy are debatable. The Freudians, led by Melanie Klein, associate envy with the death pulsion, whose origins would be innate. Freud in 1908[38], in his article "The Sexual Theories of Children" mentions the interest that girls have for the penis of the boys, interest guided by envy. But only in 1914, "Introduction to Narcissism" [39], he coined the term "penis envy", designating the complex of castration in a child of the female sex. In 1920[40], with the publication of "Beyond the pleasure principle", Freud postulates that functioning of the psychic apparatus is based on the opposition between two basic pulsations: life and death. The pulsation of death would be omnipresent, would appear generally merged with the pulsation of life, and would manifest itself in various ways, such as: compulsion to repetition, negative therapeutic reaction, aggressiveness, envy, destructive narcissism, etc.

For Melanie Klein (1974), the origins of envy are innate and derive from constitutional aggression. An excessive load of precocious envy represents a particularly malign and disastrous form of innate aggression. Primarily, the child would be envious of the breast, and later, and by displacement, she would encompass the breast-penis equation, symbols of life. With a greater integration of the ego and the appearance of guilt and the desire of reparation, envy tends to give in to gratitude. Whereas

---

38 FREUD, Sigmund. **On the sexual theories of children.** *In:* _________. Complete work. Madrid: Editorial Biblioteca Nueva, p. 1262, 1908.
39 _________. **On narcissism:** an introduction. *In:* _________. Complete work. Madrid: Editorial Biblioteca Nueva, p. 2017, 1914.
40 _________. **Beyond the pleasure principle.** Madrid: Editorial Biblioteca Nueva, p. 2507, 1920.

envy spoils the fruition of the object through the desire to destroy it, gratitude is the contrary, "the fundament of the appreciation of what is good in the others and in him/herself" (CINTRA and FIGUEIREDO, 2004, p. 133).

The neo-Freudians, like Karen Horney, Donald Woods Winnicott and Dave Hiles, emphasize less the importance of biological forces over personality, and highlight the impact of social and psychological forces. They also minimize the importance of infantile sexuality and Oedipus' complex, suggesting that the development of the personality is determined mainly by psychosocial forces and not psychosexual ones.

Karen Horney (1967)[41] argues that "penis envy", as described by Freud means only envy of masculine power in the patriarchal societies. She proposes the concept of" uterus envy", suggesting that men would envy the feminine capacity to generate lives.

Winnicott (1975)[42] believes that the newly-born does not experience, by nature, any overflowing or pulsional conflicts; he/she only has basic needs that have to be met by a good enough mother.

Dave Hiles (2007)[43], a psychotherapist from the Tavistock clinic, revisits the Kleinian theory and translates it into light of the love and hatred dynamics in the relationships. The human child is born in a state of semi-parasitism, totally dependent on his/her caretakers, especially of the mother who feeds him/her. All his/her actions and reactions are directed to have his/her mother for him/herself, including his/her reactions of hatred; this would be a form to draw the mother's attention and have her around to manage to survive. The child does not want to destroy the mother but control her presence.

For the childreen, envy is not a gratuitous aggression towards everything that is good, but a fragile response before privation, the belief that what he/she needs is being refrained by someone who does not want to give it to him/her. The resulting rage would be an effort to induce the mother to realize her desires, not to destroy her. David Hiles cites Ian Suttie (1935)[44], a Scottish psychiatrist, prior to Melanie Klein, and inspirer of ideas of Bowlby (2004)[45], who contested the Freudian sexual theory, and for whom the greatest challenge of human development is to become independent of the mother, and rage, hatred, jealousy, envy, take place when this challenge is not reached.

---

41 HORNEY, Karen. **Feminine Psychology**. Norton, p. 1922-37, 1967.
42 WINNICOTT, Donald W. **Playing and reality.** Oxfordshire: Routledge, 1975.
43 HILES, Dave R. **Envy, Jealousy, Greed: A Kleinian approach.** Paper presented to CCPE, London, 2007.
44 SUTTIE, Ian. **The origins of love and hate.** New York: Routledge, 1935.
45 BOWLBY, John. **Attachment and loss.** New York: Basic Books, 2004.

5.   Evolutionary Function of Envy

From an evolutionary perspective, envy is seen as an important instrument in the struggle for a competitive advantage (HILL and BUSS, 2006). The basic concept of Charles Darwin's Theory of Natural Selection is that favorable characteristics that are hereditary become more common in successive generations of a population of organisms that reproduce themselves, and that unfavorable characteristics, which are also hereditary, become less common.

The process of natural selection is inherently competitive. The primitive man struggled for food, shelter, warmth and, if someone had these resources and he did not, he would do anything to obtain them, on the account of his survival. We are phylogenetically equipped, in order to observe each other and compete, and we manifest these attributes in our social interactions. We continuously struggle to acquire resources or positions that the others simultaneously are struggling to get. This occurs with physical appearance, as we acquire perishable goods and even when we profess ideologies, beliefs.

The use of social comparison is a survival instrument through which human beings can evaluate if they are at advantage or disadvantage in the battle of natural selection. Therefore, envy would serve the function to warn when a rival partner is at an advantage and would push the individual in question to try and get that advantage for himself.

The negative affection felt when one perceives the advantage of the others results from an internal alarm that signals that we are losing the competition (which, in primitive times, would mean death for us and our as if an injustice were happening and try to re-establish their well-being in several ways. Many friendships are broken because one of the partners is at disadvantage and prefers to keep away from this feeling.

To keep envy in secret is also a defense strategy, since admitting its existence may only maximize other people's merits and would make it impossible to use other strategies, like gossiping to demoralize the other, saying it was unfair, etc.

6.   When does envy take place?

Every explanatory theory about envy has its way to predict when an episode of this feeling will take place. Psychoanalysts, in general, believe that envy is directly related with the experience of primary childcare. That is because the sense of having attributes, commonly called self-esteem, is opposed to being completely impotent, without attributes, without self-esteem.

A Kleinian therapist Kate Barrows (2002, p. 65-7)[46] says that envy occurs more often in certain types of relationships, in which questions related to how things are given and received are raised. If a person giving something does it in a cordial way, without belittling or humiliating, the person receiving tends to feel grateful and will return something out of gratitude. On the other hand, if the person giving does not like to do it or makes it clear that he/she is only giving because the other person wants it, this individual will feel offended, resented, inferior and may become envious. The individual does not feel free to appreciate what was given to him/her.

In his brilliant article, "Envy and its transformations", Richard Smith (2004) summarizes the four conditions for envy to take place:

1. Any envy episode starts with the observation of an attribute in another person that we wish to have.
2. The envied person is symmetric to us in many aspects: age, socio-economic level, etc. This similarity generates a sensation of injustice, "if we are equal, we should have the same things".
3. The attribute that the other possesses is of a relevant domain for us.
4. Our personal perspectives to obtain this attribute are very scarce.

To summarize, we want to have what the other person has, what our basic similarities suggest that we should have and what would be fair for us to have, but we come to the conclusion that it is beyond our reach. All these characteristics are necessary for the onset of envy. If, for instance, the object of comparison is not relevant to us, we may admire it in the other without feeling the pain of envy; if there is a low similarity of attributes, for example, the person we look up to is older, we may think reasonably that when we grow older, we will also have that quality. If we

---

46 BARROWS, Kate. **Envy**. USA: Icon Books, p. 65-7, 2002.

believe that we are able to get that quality, we will feel motivated and we will fight to obtain it and, again we won't feel the pain of envy.

Once the four conditions are met, the envy episode will take place, evolve and produce several other emotions (paranoia, resentment, shame) dispelling the initial sensation of envy. For instance, if the focus of comparison is directed to an inferiority of skills, we may feel ashamed of this inferiority, and begin to morally censure the person in question, blaming him/her for dishonesty. This diverts the focus of our recognized inferiority and justifies our acting hostilely against the envied person. "Merit envies the results", according to Montaldi's suggestion, cited by Smith (2004).

Some people, aware of their envy, decide to work hard to make up for the disadvantage and make it smaller. This is probably the most honorable way to cope with this feeling. Conversely, others remain stuck in the feeling of inferiority produced by envy and may fall into depression. It is reasonable to think that a badly resolved envy lies at the bottom of psychopathological cases.

Another configuration that envy might take is the use of slander, gossip, or indirect sabotage to undermine the qualities of the envied person. Gaiarsa (1978) explores this territory and states that chitchat, intrigue, gossip, are means of social control frequently provoked by envy. He calls "emotional pest" this surreptitious form used by envious individuals, once they cannot admit their real motivation.

Avi Berman (2007, p. 17-32)[47], a clinical contemporary psychologist and group therapist of Israel, based on his observation of children, thinks that envy contains a component of hope, a desire to have the same qualities. This author proposes three factors that may distinguish those who tend to feel resentful and destructive when they are envious from those who find self-accomplishment and motivation in these unfavorable situations. The first factor refers to the awareness of envy and may admit this feeling. The second factor refers to self-esteem and above all to a self-evaluation of one's own capacities. The third factor comprises how far the person reckons he is entitled to those qualities.

According to him, people who benefit from situations involving envy are those who admit the feeling, believe in their capacity and think they are equally deserving. However, those who suffer with this feeling and become aggressive and destructive are those who do not recognize envy, feel incapable and think they deserve much more than their rivals.

---

47 BERMAN, Avi. **Envy, competition and gender:** theory, clinical applications and group work. London: Routledge, 2007.

7. Self-esteem, competitiveness, envy and gender.

Competitiveness, self-esteem and envy appear correlated in almost all the texts that I read for this article. If we think of envy as an adaptive emotion that makes us compete to survive, even so the theorists of human emotion development would have to explain to us how we learn to compete, or yet how we learn to evaluate our real capacities so we can compare with our rivals.

If a person assesses him/herself wrongly, he/she will compete wrongly. There is no use having many attributes if the inner sensation is of depreciation and points toward deficiencies. How do we incorporate the notion of what are our real capacities, our self-value, our self-esteem?

Moreover, each culture imbues its citizens with values that condition the criteria for being accepted and valued or not. Our historically patriarchal culture has changed visibly, but some subtle traces take many generations to really settle down. Carol GILLIGAN, (1982) in her book "A Different Voice", shows that even today there are still different competitive ways for men and women. Men are still raised for growing separation from the others and reaching autonomy and independence, whereas from women one expects that, above all, they look after the relationships and be friendly and faithful.

If a man is competitive, powerful and successful, he is still in accordance with the expectations we hold from him, while a powerful, self-sufficient and well-succeeded woman is often threatened to be abandoned by her peers, as if she were a traitor, walking the other direction.

Psychoanalysis also explains this issue, showing that in phases of individuation-separation from the mother toward other relationships and autonomy, boys do not experience conflicts of the kind. If everything goes smoothly, they follow toward the identification with the father and his social roles. Girls, on the other hand, have to individuate-separate from the mother, but at the same time remain identified with their functions and social roles, which presupposes, on the contrary, non-differentiation and intimacy (CHODOROW, 1978, p.109).

Competing with the mother means separating from the complicity with her, to struggle to become different from her, better than her yet similar is a complex psychological task and carries immense pain and guilt. (LERNER, 1990). Women permeate their other relationships of gender with this conflict; which is why when a woman competes, in general, she seeks a less individualistic and more indirect formula. The win/lose of these situations is based on "everybody wins", together we win as a team (NAVARRO, 2007). Covered, passive-aggressive styles of fight, modesty and humbleness have been pre-requisites of femininity and to those acting differently, one uses not so noble adjectives, like masculine, aggressive or hysterical. (LERNER, 1990).

And what does envy have to do with this? You must be wondering. Well, if one cannot express openly what he/she wants and fights openly for what he/she needs, then he/she can only envy this capacity in the others. Envy is the best defense mechanism for an ego that has been deprived of resources and admires someone who has them. One can relieve the pain of impotence with it, utilizing not so noble hidden attitudes, such as gossip, slander, and anything that weakens his/her rival.

Although envy is a universal human phenomenon, and although it affects men and women, it is still more identified as a trace from the feminine culture, and reasonably enough, the witches that were chased and killed in the Middle Age for their evil activity were women.

8. What about the Evil Eye? Does it exist? Is it harmful?

The "Evil Eye" or "greedy eye" is the belief in which a disease is transmitted – usually unwillingly – from someone who is envious or jealous. This person, normally, is not your enemy, but feeling envious, they may harm you, your children, your animals, or your plantation, by casting an envious look. The main victims are the babies and small children because they are very much observed and praised by strangers.

In Hebrew it is "ayin há'ra" (evil eye), in Italian "mal occhio" (bad eye) and in Spanish "mal ojo". So, there are different connotations for this superstition in every language, as well as records of rituals and amulets for protection in every culture, from the tribal societies to our times of global society. For example, there are reports about envy in the Sumerian writings from 4000 years B.C. (LANGDON, 1981) and in the sarcophagus in Egypt, in the XXI and XXII centuries B.C. (ROJAS-BERMUDEZ, 1998)[48], there are drawings of eyes symbolizing acting and negative energies (see Table 1).

In the Oriental Mediterranean and in the Aegean Sea region, especially in the whole of Greece and even in Turkey, there is a strong tendency to see blue-eyed people as carrying the "bad eye", probably because few people have blue eyes in these regions.

In Greece and in Turkey, a glass or porcelain blue eye and a Hamsa hand – mystic artifact showing the palm of the hand with five

---

48 Rojas-Bermúdez, J. (1998)- De La Invídia y de La Violencia- em Revista da Sociedade Portuguesa de Psicodrama, nº 5, Lisboa, Portugal.

fingers stretched out – are usually displayed in necklaces and in jewelry, as if to face the "blue eye of envy". In Christian countries, making the sign of the cross or a "figa" with the fingers (a gesture using a special crossing of the fingers) seems to be the mostly used antidote.

Alan Dundes made a multicultural study of the talismans and healings against the "evil eye" and he noticed some common features. It seems that the harm caused by the look is often connected to symptoms of dryness and dehydration, as if the look were a kind of microwave and many rituals for the healing usually involve humidity. I concluded that the belief in the evil eye is just another way that human beings have found to deal with the enigma of life and death, consisting of creating metaphors and rituals to keep the living humid in opposition to the dead, dry of all the vital fluids. We can see a typical example in the fish used by the Japanese as an antidote against envy because they are always wet. Also, among the Jew, it is a habit to spit at both sides of the envied person.

Who are the envious ones?	Those who praise the children; those who are envious; those who have blue eyes; women with no children, the people who are born with the tendency of, without realizing, cast the envious eye.
Who are the victims and their symptoms?	Breastfeeding mothers who get sick and cry; the mother's milk may dry, young people who get sick and may vomit or become apathic; cows and sheep whose milk dry; fruit trees that wither and die or don't produce fruit; orphan children or parents who lost their children; adult men who become impotent.
Rituals to prevent envy	Refusal in accepting praise for the child; spit on the child; smear of rust or dirt on the child for him/her not to get pretty; protective sentences and gestures; make the gesture of "figa", (special crossing of the fingers) make the sign of the cross; the oil running in water and prayer; wax running in water and prayer; live coal or match heads falling in the water and prayer; touch the face with an intact raw egg, breaking it afterwards; break an egg inside a dark hidden tube; break an egg and draw the sign of the cross on the victim's forehead; throw an egg in the woods or against a tree (if the tree is the victim); put a broken egg on

	the victim's plate or under his/her bed; victim drinks three gulps of blessed water; victim is bathed in blessed water; spit three times on the victim; water or saliva is spread on the victims mouth; collecting saliva from the group (anonymous donation) to spread on the victim, etc.
Amulets	Protective hand, jewelry such as the eye that sees everything; Buda's eye; glass eye; enchantment mirror; fumigation with seeds; aspand (a herb from Zoroastro's time) burned in vegetal coal; magic reciting; red thread; or a red coral necklace; buckle with Issis amulets; horseshoes.

TABLE 1- ENVY OBJECTS, CURSINGS AND AMULETS

According to Freud's (1901, p. 919) point of view, the belief in the "bad eye" is a superstition and as such, it represents the fear of future misfortunes. Besides, the fear that people "wish us harm" would be the conscious manifestation of the unconscious repression of our own bad wishes against others. However, it is necessary to remember that despite being superstitious, this belief has the power of suggestion that cannot be undervalued.

The superstitions are ideas absorbed from the environment. They are emotionally linked to the potent and primitive tendency, either instinctive or ancestral, of reacting with great fear to everything which may have any relation to supernatural powers. Such a tendency, clearly expressed in the child and in the primitive man, continues latent in the civilized adult, being about to emerge in critical situations even in people with high cultural level.

From Franz Anton Mesmer (1734 - 1815) - who, using his animal magnetism, healed pains and illnesses by applying magnets to the forehead of people - to Jean Martin Charcot, (1825 - 1893) the hypnotizer of the hysterical women - and Freud – who abandoned the hypnosis concluding that it was just the power of suggestion -, culminating with the contemporary cognitive therapies (BECK and KUYKEN, 2003), we know that the beliefs we have about ourselves, about the world and about the future, determine the way we feel and how we behave, deeply affecting our well-being.

So, yes, the "evil eye" is harmful. Both envied and envious are damaged by believing in this superstition: the envious one for believing that they are inferior to the person with whom they compare to and for obsessively losing their time and creativity trying to control the envied one. As to the person who believes having been infected by the "evil eye", will also present, for the power of suggestion, the corresponding harm and will feel impelled to perform a ritual for healing.

9. Marketing and envy: the power and the danger of being envied

Most of the studies about envy focus their observation on the envious person. The target of envy, the person who is envied or who makes themselves envied, is scarcely studied. Having qualities, facilities in life, being in an outstanding position cause various sensation, from power to guilt, discomfort, and fear that something bad is about to happen.

The Greeks, according to Helmut Shoeck (1987, p. 141-52), mentioned the Gods' envy in several myths, as if there were a divine justice in the distribution of wealth with a guaranteed punishment for those who dare trespass the limits. In the same line of reasoning, we can see the idea that the pleasure is prohibited in many religions or at least taxed with the tithing that proceeds with the redistributive justice and still, all the rituals of knocking on wood, making the sign of the cross, etc., every time we realize that something good is happening.

In a capitalist society, where consumption is encouraged by aggressive marketing which overuses the comparison among people, we are instigated to envy something all the time. We envy the car which is attractively offered on TV by a woman even more beautiful than the car, who is clothed and accessorized more beautifully than her and the car and, above all, who is being photographed at a paradisiacal place, much better than the car, the model, the clothes and the accessories.

Being the target of someone's envy grants this person a status of power and the reassuring of their own value. It predisposes them to receive aggressive acts, either direct or indirect (such as moral devaluation, gossip, sabotage, etc.), and an uncomfortable feeling of guilt for being the involuntary cause of someone's suffering.

As well as the consumer, the target of the advertisement exemplified above, when we are compared to people who have attributes (objects, beauty, qualities, etc.) superior to ours, we feel attacked in our self-esteem, which demands a retaliation action to recover our value. Making yourself envied may be an aggressive act, because envy is a social emotion and affects, not only isolated individuals, but also groups.

George Foster (1972) suggests that there are two ways to analyze envy: from the competitive point of view, it is useful to be envied; as in the point of view of fear of retaliation, it is safer not to be perceived and conceal your qualities.

Dealing with somebody else's envy is a complex task. The studies in social psychology suggest some strategies commonly used to deal with envious people:

1. Minimize our own qualities.
2. Value the effort we had to make to achieve these qualities.
3. Praise the person who envies us, trying to point out their qualities.
4. Help the one who envies us, trying to give them something good.
5. Conceal our qualities under a fake humbleness, modesty.
6. Socialize our profits, showing how our qualities help other people.

Being envied, after all, is an ambiguous existential position. At the same time in which it represents a solitary way of reassuring, surplus value, it may end up producing relationship isolation, a lack of harmonious peers with whom one could share joy.

10. The envy in psychodramatic literature

I have found only one text dedicated to envy in our national and international psychodramatic world. It was Rojas-Bermudez's (1997) paper, "De la envidia y de la violencia". Rojas-Bermudez studies the relation between envy and violence, concluding that violence is the result of lack of resources of the self to elaborate the envy provoked by the other. He conceives envy as a natural aspect of the human being, like hunger and thirst, but it is insatiable, as a consequence, its tragedy (sic). It is unleashed by a social fact, meeting someone whose virtues make our limitations evident. Says the author: (1998, p. 53):

"Envy is an emotional response that emerges due to previous existing lack of affection and that gets established as passion".

To elaborate it depends on one's intra-psychic resources, values and intellectual possibilities to transform this suffering into creativity and compensate for the lack of affection. If they fail, they will first try to fight against this passion and later, cast their energy against the source of their passion - the other, the envied one - beginning the violence.

Moreno did not directly study the phenomenon of human envy, he only mentioned it occasionally in his work, although he referred to several questions relevant to the theme, through the sociometric test. He mentions, for example, "the creator's envy", referring to the rivalry existing among creative people, either heroes, scientists, or revolutionaries - rivalry that could even be evaluated through the citations the authors of scientific papers make about their colleagues:

This phenomenon was named "the creator's envy". People like him, pioneers of the ones who perform the position of "public-relations" in our illuminated era, may have appeared frequently in the course of history, heroes of the people, acting simultaneously as anti-geniuses and geniuses (...). There have often been rival geniuses in conflict with each other; the fire was stolen from each generation and so, gradually the scientific methodology was developed. (he refers to the myth of Prometheus) (MORENO, 1992, v.1, p. 135).
I used a cold sociometrics (cold because it is frozen in books). (ibidem).

Moreno even seems to believe this competitiveness is positive for science, despite being painful for the sociometric stars that may be rejected by their pioneers. He says: "the creator's envy phenomenon also has good social characteristics; it helped the scientific method to be released" (ibidem, p.140). The psychodramatic production revealed intense hostility, being reinforced by one of the two key-individuals and rivals, sometimes resulting in a distorted perception of the pioneer and of their work.

"The chain reaction has produced social network denial which may be called antipathy for the pioneer, or 'creator's envy'". (ibidem, p. 136-7).

Moreno also understood the sociometric power of envy, which through direct or indirect boycott, may relegate creative geniuses to ostracism.

To exalt or to blame, to steal or despise silently, to cite occasionally or not to cite the work of a genius is a dynamic way of determining their fortunate career. (ibidem, p. 139).

As to social revolutions and their real motivations, hidden behind ideologies, Moreno wisely perceived the importance that the feeling of envy has when the disputes involve merit matters versus justice matters[49]. He says about Nazism:

If, as it is stated, Jews in Germany have a disproportionate situation, according to their numerical importance, in liberal professions, in arts, in industry, this may be due to an excessive effort from them, maybe bigger than the effort made by the Germans, equally talented. In this case, there are currents both aggressive and protective, in the attempt of balancing conditions that seem to threaten the strength of certain elements from the majoritarian group (MORENO, 1992, v.3, p. 128).

As the majority of the dependent groups are German, we can imagine the rage coming up among German groups of leaders, feelings that are joined to the belief that they have more "natural rights" than the Jewish leaders to lead the masses of workers and German farmers (ibidem, p. 130).

---

49 In fact, the matter of envy is mixed with interrogations about merit and justice: the one who has the merits to have the attributes is not necessarily the one who, for right or justice (changeable according to the period in history), has them. The political fights try to change the laws, to minimize the feeling of difference and injustice. Ironically, it will appear again, in the lower level of the new resulting hierarchy, wrapped up in another demagogic ornament.

From Moreno's understanding, it was his aim to give relevance to the power a human being has above the other, the importance of being appreciated and accepted, not only in the first affective relationships, but also, in all the relationships throughout life. He has always been interested in the rejected minorities, in the sociometric proletariats[50] (1992, p. 225) trying to re-integrate them in a certain group. He has done this through sociometry, especially through the Sociometric Test, whose basic proposal was to allow people to choose the relationships and the groups where they wanted to study, work and live.

He did not dedicate directly to the matter of self-esteem or narcissism in any moment of his work. He did not do it probably because of the emphasis he has always given to the relationship aspects instead of intra-psychic matters. The closest he got to reflecting the matter of the self with itself, was the formulation of the concept of *"autotele"* (MORENO, 1992, p. 140), used for speaking about the relationship of the child with themselves and with their image, and about the collapse of the psychotics' self-image.

Sometimes, Moreno seems to refer to the notion of personal value, but the term he uses is "status". He mentions, for example, "sociometric status" (1974, p. 234-5; 1992, v.3, p. 194-7), referring to the total of choices the individual has in a group; "status of the men in the cosmic order" (1984, p. 24) about the commotion the Copernican discoveries represented for men's pride.

Due to the resistances (1992, p. 202-3) brought about by the sociometric test, Moreno perceives that there is a fear in exposing the relationship preferences. Referring to the sociometric procedures, he states:

(...) the resistance seems paradoxical at first, since it appears in opposition to the real opportunity of having a basic necessity fulfilled. This resistance of the individual against the group can be explained. It is on one hand, the fear that the individual has of knowing their position in the group. Becoming aware of this position, either by themselves or through others, may be painful and unpleasant. Another source of resistance is the fear that it may become apparent to other people we like or even the ones we do not like and which would be the position in the

---

50 Moreno uses the concept of sociometric proletariat to speak about the isolated groups, neglected and rejected, whose feelings do not find reciprocity

group that we really want and need. The resistance is produced by the extra-individual situation of an individual, by the position they have in the group. They feel that their position in the group does not result from individual efforts. It is mainly the result of how the individuals with whom they live feel about them. They may even feel, slightly, that besides his social atom there are invisible tele structures influencing their position. The fear of expressing the preferential feelings that one person has for the others, is in fact, the fear of the feelings that the others... have for them (...).

(...) These procedures should be favorably welcomed, since they help in the recognition and comprehension of the basic structure of the group. However, this is not the case. They find resistance and even hostility from some people (...).

(...) Other individuals also expressed fear of the revelations that the sociometric procedure could bring. The fear is more intense in some people and less intense in others. Some may be more anxious to arrange their relationships according to their present wishes, others are afraid of the consequences (...). These and other facts reveal a fundamental phenomenon, the interpersonal resistance, resistance against expressing the preferential feelings that some have for the others (MORENO, v.3, p. 153-4).

As to the social differences and the injustice regarding the distribution of wealth and qualities, the Morenian concept of sociodynamic effect seems to describe this process. According to him we are different and this differentiation is detected and partially softened by the sociometric procedures. However, it would be utopic to imagine absolutely egalitarian societies (ibidem, p. 195).
The hypothesis of the sociodynamic effect states that:

Some individuals from a certain group will be persistently excluded from productive communication and social contact.
Some individuals are constantly neglected, very much below their expectations and others are very much favored, in a disproportional way to their demands.

Conflicts and tensions come up in the groups as the sociodynamic effect grows, in other words, with the growing polarity between the favored and the neglected. As the sociodynamic effect is reduced – reduction of the polarity between favored and neglected – the conflicts and the tensions are reduced. However, questions emerged about the possibility of having a society without sociodynamic effect, if such a society has ever existed or if it will exist in the future and if it would be superior to the present one. Many religious societies have tried to eliminate the differential trait from the group, through the suppression of perceptions and differential feelings in their minds, according to their system of values that assume all the men are brothers and equal, children of God. Therefore, the differentiation becomes a mortal sin, and sociometrics, the devil's science. Another possibility would be to accept the sociodynamic effect as our destiny.

11. My opinion

Envy is a universal human phenomenon, timeless and inevitable. It is part of the structure of the human psyche and it operates in the human culture and in our social organization. However, the way of dealing with this feeling varies according to the emotional balance and the self-evaluation that each one of us makes about our qualities, capacities and merits facing the circumstances of life.
In my book, Emotional Survival (CUKIER, 1998), I developed the idea that the different aspects of our identity, or in the terms of Moreno's role theory, our different relationship possibilities, are organized according to a kind of "system of self-esteem maintenance". I believe that from the first dependency relationships, the central role of our identity is structured. The value the "self" acquires at this first evaluation will determine the compensatory maneuvers that it will have to make to maintain its narcissism at tolerable levels.
In the beginning of intrauterine life, the child does not know where the pleasure and displeasure come from. They experiment psychosomatic roles[51] as an indiscriminate whole – the child, the world, the mother and

---

51 MORENO (1975) says "The first roles to appear are the physiological or psychosomatic". We know that between the sexual role, the role of the individual who sleeps, of the one who dreams and of the one who eats, operational bonds are developed which link these roles and integrate them in a unit. At a certain point we could

the breast, the child and the colic, the colic and the mother. Just little by little, as the neurological system matures and through the repetition of the experience, the child begins to associate the pleasure with the presence of the mother or provider and the displeasure with her absence (this referring to a normal child, with normally providing parents).

In other words, what initially was decoded as pleasurable because it satiated a survival physiological necessity, begins to acquire certain independence and it does not need the physiological necessity to occur (FREUD, 1905, p. 1119-200).[52] The presence of the mother and/or provider(s) begins to produce, even when there is no necessity to be satisfied. It is the pleasure of being seen, touched, looked after, listened to by someone who potentially is more powerful and that grants me a certain power if they choose to be with me. The opposite is also true, the experience of displeasure begins to exist each time the provider does not show up or shows up but does not give all the attention the subject expects.

This new kind of pleasure – displeasure is what will constitute what I call "Narcissistic Economy"[53] or "system of self-esteem maintenance", a second system within the psyche, joined to what regulates the pleasure and displeasure of the body, responsible for determining, all the time, the value of the "self" for the other (how much the other likes the "self") and for themselves (self-esteem).

We all know from our own experience that there is pain that is not physical, but psychological. The self-esteem needs to be maintained within certain levels of value, otherwise pain is produced – it is the pain

---

consider this unit as a kind of physiological self, a "partial" self, a conglomerate of physiological roles.

52 FREUD (1905) in "Three Essays on the Theory of Sexuality", develops the theory that in the origin, the first sexual satisfactions appear by the time of the functioning of the organs that are meant to preserve life. He speaks about object anaclitical choice, showing how the sexual pulsations are based on the self-preserving ones. I think that not only is sexual satisfaction based on these first experiences of pleasure-displeasure, but also the narcissistic satisfaction of perceiving oneself as the target of attention and value from others.

53 The use of the term "Narcissistic Economy" is analogical, it uses the idea of self-interest (Narcissus who only thinks about himself), but also the idea of homeostasis or economy, showing the self-protective function of this mechanism in the psyche. The pleasure in this narcissistic system is achieved when the individual's self-esteem is high and the displeasure or narcissistic pain, when self-esteem is low.

of not being loved, the pain of perceiving yourself of little importance for the other, the pain of feeling vulnerable, the pain of feeling deceived, betrayed - and also the pain of envy, feeling that another one has attributes that you wanted for yourself. This is what Kohut (1972, v.2, p. 615-58) calls *narcissistic injury* – the sudden perception that the self thought to be valued by others or by themselves, in fact may abruptly lose this power.

The criteria for the self to feel valued or not, vary according to parameters stated by the family and socio-cultural environment from which the subject emerges, they are relative criteria and somewhat flexible, because they change according to the development, the moment in life. However, two rules, extremely simple to be formulated, coordinate the central structure of this value system, one inter-relational and the other one intrapsychic:

1. As *inter-relational*, I understand all the relationships that one person establishes with other people, from the first relationships with the mother and family members to the most complex adult relationships. This way, every time the self feels valued by another, gratuitously or for something they have done, their intrinsic value and self-esteem heighten; the opposite is also true and the person feels devalued when they do not get the desired attention;

2. The *intrapsychic* one consists of the relationships one person maintains with themselves, and in this context the rule for the self to know if they have or do not have value is even more simple: the self likes itself when liked and cannot tolerate itself if felt rejected or despised.

Each person probably has an optimum level of personal value that their psyche needs to maintain in order to psychologically survive. When this self-value or self-esteem is very low, defensive resources are created to try to optimize it, through certain strength compensation. The violence originated by the pain of envy would be one of these defensive maneuvers, which tries to compensate for our self-value in the presence of the superiority we perceive in the other.

Therefore, to work therapeutically with envy, implies reviewing the client's emotional life and their narcissism. It is a task that begins from a present conflict, but goes through the client's life, making use of dramatic associations and the tracing of repetitions and transferences (CUKIER, 1998, p. 69-76). The final objective is to promote repairing in the patient's self-esteem maintaining system, or narcissistic system that, as I explained before, consists of a kind of central self-evaluation - or in Morenian terms, a permanent central socio-autometric - that we have in our psyche and which informs us all the time what is our value is for the other and for ourselves.

12. How do we work psycho-dramatically with envy?

In general, the theme envy appears indirectly through relational conflicts or, more often, through the client's observation that the others envy them. I have never received a case in which the person identified their problem as an excess of envy, for the shame this statement would promote. For this reason, I think we must work this matter in an indirect way, also following the client's clues. The psychodrama offers us many resources to advance, from the present scenes of a relational conflict, to the intra-psychic drama, where themes such as self-esteem and narcissism are cleared up. The work with regressive scenes (CUKIER, 1998, p. 69-76) and their present repercussions is, in my opinion, the most profound in this case.

Maybe what is more difficult, is to begin the warming up for the patient to be willing to approach the theme of envy. One can do this in a subtle way, using the inversion of roles every time the demand comes in the way of: "the other envies me". In this case, the patient is asked to be this other one, put themselves in their attitude, experiment life a little as if they were the envied one. This inversion should be explored deeply, especially the feeling of rage that the rival's attributes cause to the client. The inversion of roles also allows the client to experiment the theme of the envy from both sides: being the envied and the envious. In both roles we can ask for associations with situations already lived and deepen the psychodynamic.

The interpolation of a sculpture of this conflicting relationship is very useful to work this theme from a distance. I had a client that complained about how much her very rich sister-in-law envied her commitment to work and to fight for life. When playing the sister-in-law's role, I asked her to tell me how the wealth could be seen in her way of being, if it was in her clothes, attitude, etc. The client immediately began to describe in detail the clothing brands, her stylists made purses, her shopping at Daslu (a fashionable Brazilian boutique), etc. Her attitude was majestic, she moved like a queen. I asked her, still in the sister-in-law's role, to talk about my client, and the first thing she said was: "she is poor, she dresses badly, goes shopping on José Paulino (a popular shopping street)". Next, I asked the client to look at this relationship from a distance and create a clay sculpture of two people who interact like this. What would this sculpture be like? Which attitude would the rich have and which attitude would the poor have? Afterwards, I asked her to name the sculpture. The name she chose was: the slave and the queen.

The theme of the slave and the queen was the main point of this client's whole therapy and she gradually faced her feeling of inferiority in childhood. Many scenes were dramatized - scenes at her elementary school, where she always had to borrow the school material because her parents could not afford it; scenes at family meals, where there was not meat for everyone and the parents did not eat it, causing the children to feel guilty – after all, scenes where she learned not to wish what she could not have and to hate people who had them.

Understanding the child's pain and impotence and learning neither to surrender to them nor making use of the same former defenses, the client was able to perceive that she was an adult, she earned a good salary and could give herself things, objects and comforts that she would like to have. In the last therapy session, she brought a purse, by a famous brand, saying that it had been a present for herself after having had the courage of looking at her life. We never mentioned the word envy during her therapeutic process and her sister-in-law disappeared gradually from her conflicts.

The technique of the double is inadvisable for the theme of envy. Telling a client that they feel envious is almost like slapping their face, the opposite idea from a subtle work. However, the mirror favors a look from a distance of the conflict and is a great therapeutic aid. In the case reported above, many insights were obtained when the client, looking from a distance the scene that she had just played with the sister-in-law, remembered another scene, in another context, in which she also felt like a slave. The mirror favors the perception of the transferential chain.

Metaphors, maximizations, concretizations, drama games, are all useful and desirable action possibilities especially in group psychodrama, where the theme of envy comes up *in situ*, involving all the participants of the group, even the therapist and the auxiliary ego. There were some group situations that happened often in my clinic, in which a certain client would resent the attention that I, as a therapist, had given to another client. Mixed with this open jealousy, I have often seen, after some work, feelings of inferiority in relation to the rival, associations to situations of the immediate family emerge.

The magical store, where the client symbolically buys different kinds of characteristics, at the same time they sell or exchange character traits or personality, is usually useful to clarify what is envied in the other.

A very important aspect in therapeutic work with envy is to help the client go through the mourning of the world's ideal of justice, to accept the unfair reality of life. Equally important is to accept the feeling of envy, without disqualifying themselves, perceiving that it is a human emotion, but that it should neither become an obsession, nor lead to revenging actions or hatred. The client also needs to legitimate the desire that is implicit in the envy and take actions to obtain it. The role-playing technique is very good to learn how to test new roles, attitudes, wishes, etc.

Finally, I should say that an efficient therapy for envy helps the client to reduce their shame, heighten their self-value, look at their own desires and be open to the richness of life. Less physical strength will be used to compare to others, and more will be used to have compassion for themselves and for everyone who fights to have the best life they can.

Conclusions

My first intuition in wanting to study human envy would say that this so hidden and shameful feeling was directly or indirectly related to severe psychopathological episodes, such as the psychosis and the borderline episodes. In fact, a clinical experience of more than 30 years is the basis for this intuition. I have always found, in approaching the intrapsychic of severe episodes, matters related to self-esteem, apparently unapproachable and, many times, the self-deprecation originated from the fact that there had been in the lives of these clients, as well as in the lives of all of us, people with more abilities, beauty, intelligence, money, etc. I would ask myself why most of us are able to deal with these differences between human beings and try to maximize our own attributes - improve our qualities, study, work, progress -; while others among us paralyze in face of the same reality - getting obsessed by iniquities, creating supplemental realities to compensate for their lack, developing aggressive mechanisms to "make justice by their own hands" or, desperately have a self-destructive behavior at the impossibility of this undertaking?

Another fact that became evident in my *clinic is* that pointing out the client's feelings of envy, with some exceptions, unleashes negative reactions, sometimes aggressive and of disharmony between therapist and client. In other words, it is impossible to approach envy in a direct and frank way. So, I developed several resources to work with this matter without ever mentioning the word that could come up or not, in the therapeutic process.

However, I remained curious about this great taboo that was so frequent in the clinic. This work has come to satiate this curiosity and provided me with some conclusions:

Envy is a universal and timeless human phenomenon. It is part of the human psyche and operates in human culture and in social organization. Opposite to the equivalent feeling of emulation[54], which leads the individual to try to be equal or overcome the other, it paralyzes the one who feels it and makes him/her suffer.

This suffering is the consequence of the perception of a lack or disadvantage, felt as unfair and demanding impossible repairing actions, unless they are achieved through direct or indirect violence (destroying the rival, social revolutions, boycott, gossip, etc.).

The pain and the violence resulting from this process are proportional to the dysfunctions in the client's earlier emotional development. In other words, the less developed and differentiated their personality, the more dysfunctional their original family had been, the worse their self-evaluation, self-esteem; the greater will be the damages in the perception of their disadvantage.

Naming it directly to the client causes shame and maximizes the underlying feelings of inferiority. It is necessary to use an indirect way of working which allows access to a relaxed ground.

---

54 Houaiss, A- (2001) - Dicionário Houaiss da língua portuguesa, editora Objetiva, Rio de Janeiro.

REFERENCES

ARISTOTLE. Art of rhetoric. Chicago: University of Chicago Press, 2019.

BARROWS, Kate. Envy. USA: Icon Books, p. 65-7, 2002.

BECK, A. T.; KUYKEN, W. Terapia cognitiva: abordagem revolucionária. In: ABREU C. N.; ROSO M. (org.) Psicoterapias cognitiva e construtivista: novas fronteiras da prática clínica. Porto Alegre: Artes Médicas, 2003

BERMAN, Avi. Envy, competition and gender: theory, clinical applications and group work. London: Routledge, 2007.

BOWLBY, John. Attachment and loss. New York: Basic Books, 2004.

BUSTOS, D. M.(1982) *et al*. Psychodrama. Editora Summus,São Paulo, Brasil.

BYINGTON, Carlos A. B. Creative envy: the rescue of one of civilization's major forces. Chiron Publications, 2013.

CHAVES, E. O. Justiça social, igualitarismo e inveja: a propósito do livro de Gonçalo Fernandez de La Mora. Revista da Faculdade de Educação da Unicamp, n. 4, março, 1991.

CHODOROW, Nancy. The reproduction of mothering: psychoanalysis and the sociology of gender. Berkley: University of California Press, 1978.

CINTRA, Elisa; FIGUEIREDO, Luis. Melanie Klein: styles and thoughts. São Paulo: Escuta, 2004.

CUKIER, Rosa. Bipersonal Psychodrama: Its Techniques, Therapists, and Clients"? São Paulo: Editora Ágora, 1998.

DAMÁSIO, A. (2003)- Looking for Spinoza: Joy, Sorrow, and the feeling brain. Harvest, London.

DUNDES, Alan. The evil eye: a casebook. Wisconsin: University of Wisconsin Press, 1992.

FOSTER, M. G. The anatomy of envy: a study in symbolic behavior. Current Anthropology, v.13, n.2, 1972.

FRANZ ANTON MESMER. (n./d.). Wikipedia. Available at: https://en.wikipedia.org/wiki/Franz_Mesmer. Accessed in: Apr 10, 2017.

FREUD, Sigmund. On the sexual theories of children. *In:* ________. (1908) Complete Work. Madrid: Editorial Biblioteca Nueva, p. 1262, Buenos Aires.

________. (1914).On narcissism: an introduction. *In:* ________. Complete work. Madrid: Editorial Biblioteca Nueva, Buenos Aires.

________.(1920). Beyond the pleasure principle. Madrid: Editorial Biblioteca Nueva, p. 2507, Buenos Aires.

FREUD, S. (1901) Psicopatología de la vida cotidiana. In: Obras completas. Madrid: Editorial Biblioteca Nueva, Buenos Aires.

________. (1905)- Tres ensayos sobre la teoría sexual. In: Obras completas. Madrid: Editorial Biblioteca Nueva, Buenos Aires

GAIARSA, J. Tratado geral sobre a fofoca. São Paulo: Summus, 1978.

GILLIGAN, Carol. In a Different Voice: Psychological Theory and Women's Development. Massachusetts: Harvard University Press, 2016.

HILES, Dave R. Envy, Jealousy, Greed: A Kleinian approach. Paper presented to CCPE, London, 2007.

HILL, S.; BUSS, D. The evolutionary psychology of envy. *In:* SMITH, R. H. Envy. London, Oxford University Press, 2008.

HORNEY, Karen. Feminine Psychology (reprints). Norton, p. 1922-37, 1967.

JEAN-MARTIN CHARCOT. (s./d.). Wikipedia. Available at: https://en.wikipedia.org/wiki/Jean-Martin_Charcot. Accessed in: Apr 10, 2017.

JUNG, C. G. Fundamentos de psicologia analítica. Petrópolis: Vozes, 1991.

KLEIN, M. **Love, Guilt and Reparation: And Other Works** 1921-1945 (Writings of Melanie Klein) , (2002)- Free Press

KOHUT, H. Thoughts on narcissism and narcissistic rage. *In:* The search for the self. London: International Universities Press, 1972.

LA MORA, Gonzalo F. Egalitarian envy: the political foundations of social justice. New York: Paragon House Publishers, 1987.

LERNER, Harriet. Women in therapy. New York: Harper & Row, 1994.

MORENO, Jacob Levy. Psychodrama. São Paulo: Cultrix, 1975.

________. Who shall survive? Foundations of sociometry, group psychotherapy and sociodrama. New York: Beacon House.

NAVARRO, Leyla; SCHWARTZBERG, Sharan. **Envy, competition and gender.** London: Routledge, 2007.

ROJAS-BERMUDEZ, J. De la envidia y de la violencia. Revista de la Asociación Argentina de Psiquiatras, ano III, v.2, n. 2,1997.

SAPOLSKY, Robert M. **Monkeyluv:** and other essays on our lives as animals. New York: Scribner, 2005.

SCHOECK, Helmut. **Envy:** a theory of social behaviour. New York: Liberty Fund, 1987.

SHAKESPEARE, William. **Othello.** London: Routledge, 2003.

SMITH, R. H. Envy and its transmutations. *In:* TIEDENS, L. Z.; LEACH, C. W. **The social life of emotions.** Cambridge: Cambridge University Press, 2004.

SUTTIE, Ian. **The origins of love and hate.** New York: Routledge, 1935.

TAKAHASHI, H. *et al.* When your gain is my pain and your pain is my gain: neural correlates of envy and Schadenfreude. **Science,** v.323, n.5916, p. 937-9, 2009.

WINNICOTT, Donald W. **Playing and reality.** Oxfordshire: Routledge, 1975.

POST-TRAUMATIC STRESS DISORDER: CURRENT TRENDS, TREATMENT AND PSYCHODRAMA[55]

Acknowledgements
I would especially like to thank CECILIA ZYLBERSTAJN for the help with the research.

INTRODUCTION

The study of human reactions to trauma has grown substantially in recent years. What before seemed to be a rare event, addressing only Freud´s Theory of Hysteria (1914, p. 1901), now resurfaces also with warfighters, survivors of natural disasters and the generalized symptoms of anxiety in victims of child abuse and domestic violence. A greater understanding of how the human brain functions in extreme situations has been gained (CUKIER, 2004) and, despite the different origins of trauma, personal or collective, the symptoms arising from it have striking similarities: dissociative states, personality fragmentation, affective and anxious disorders, somatization, tendencies toward suicide, intrusive thoughts and images, repeating situations where there is danger and personal abuse, nightmares, insomnia, etc.

Verbal therapies are admittedly deficient (VAN DER KOLK, 2002) in these circumstances, because the prefrontal cortex does not function properly at the time of the trauma, registering sensations, rather than cognition. Body therapies are the most recommended, and Psychodrama, as we know, is one of the oldest.

On the other hand, due to the expansion of field work, numerous new therapies have appeared, each claiming greater efficiency and speed than the other, making old-school psychodynamic therapists (including psycho-dramatists) seem like old-fashioned dinosaurs with no useful resources to deal with these issues.

The aim of this paper is to show the contemporary contributions from fellow international psycho-dramatists to deal with Post-traumatic Stress Disorder (PTST), as well as encourage the development of

---

55 Work presented at the XX Brazilian Psychodrama Congress, 2016.

statistically controlled studies that can show the wealth of our theoretical and practical knowledge.

I. STATISTICAL STUDIES ON THERAPEUTIC EFFICACY IN POST-TRAUMATIC STRESS DISORDER

At first glance, a brief review of statistical studies carried out in recent years concerning the therapeutic efficacy of the various approaches to PTSD, shows a slight advantage regarding the Eye Movement Desensitization and Reprocessing (EMDR) (CARLSON *et al,* 1998) and Cognitive Behavioral Therapy (CBT) (BRYANT, 1999) approaches, especially if both techniques are adapted to focus on trauma (JONATHAN *et al.*, 2007)

Different names are used to nominate quite similar techniques: cognitive therapy (JUDITH, 2001), cognitive behavioral therapy (CORTNEY *et al.*, 2011), cognitive behavioral therapy focused on trauma (COHEN *et al.*, 2000), etc. In other words, approaches become specific to the mental disorders they study, and they create special protocols with techniques from non-specific sources

Somatic Therapy (ST) has few statistical studies but has begun to gather evidence. Gina Ross (BROM *et al.*, 2015), in an as yet unpublished study, compared 63 people in somatic therapy with a waiting list control group - both groups diagnosed with PTSD using the DSM-IV criteria. Statistical analysis showed that both PTSD and depression symptoms significantly decreased in the treatment group and remained the same in the control group.

Exposure therapy (imaginary or live) is a technique, among others, from EMDR. A review carried out in 2012 shows extensive statistics favorable to this method (RAUCH *et al.*, 2012), and a few sessions seem necessary to relieve complex symptoms (RICHARDS *et al.*, 1994). Other recent studies postulate that the method is not magic and may even worsen symptoms and retraumatize clients (BUNMI, 2009; LEE and CUIJPERS, 2015).

Since its discovery, EMDR has been considered one of the chosen treatments for PTSD. Its great novelty - bilateral stimulation of eyes, ears or skin to reunite the language of the cerebral hemispheres - is not proven to be effective (MCNALLY, 1999; PITMAN *et al.,* 1996).

Statistical assessments of the efficacy of interpersonal psychotherapies and long-term psychodynamic psychotherapies with post-traumatic stress disorder are scarcer, but show positive results (ULRICH *et al.*, 2006). A study comparing interpersonal therapy with exposure therapy for depressed clients concludes that exposure is not always beneficial and that interpersonal therapy is more effective in some cases (MARKOWITZ *et al.*, 2015). Another study concludes that there are no significant differences between cognitive therapy and psychodynamic psychotherapy in the treatment of war veterans (OFIRr *et al.*, 2015).

Concerning psychodrama, statistics are even more scarce. A meta-analysis based on 25 experimental studies, with different pathologies, indicates a very positive result when compared to psychotherapy groups in general. The techniques of role reversal and doubling were the most effective interventions (KIPPER and RITCHIE, 2003). Empirical research has shown that experiential psychotherapy can be very effective in post-traumatic stress disorder (ELLIOT *et al.*, 1996, 1998).

As can be observed, there are considerable controversies in this field. Complex decisions about the study design need to be made: which statistical method to use, how to standardize the sampling, advantages and disadvantages of using control groups, pre and post-treatment assessments, meta-analysis to obtain more reliable generalizations and, finally, longitudinal studies that prove the permanence of therapeutic success.

Nonetheless, scientifically proven therapeutic methods are considered more effective and are more recommended, especially considering public health policies that favor short-term results. Thus, the therapies less studied in the treatment of PTSD, including psychodrama, end up being marginalized.

II. POST-TRAUMATIC STRESS DISORDER AND PSYCHODRAMA

Trauma interrupts and prevents defense responses of the organism, freezing cognitive functions and leaving the body terrified, unprotected. Verbal therapies are inefficient, and body mobilization is necessary to try to rescue muscle power and restore cognitive functions.

Psychodrama was one of the first body therapies and its only disadvantage is that it is a theoretical body of knowledge which has not been evaluated much, statistically speaking. Considering this concern of systematizing psychodramatic work and showing its effectiveness, Kellerman and Hudgins (2010) compiled technical suggestions in a magnificent book from various authors concerning post-traumatic stress disorder.

Kellerman (1992) shows six technical strategies of psychodrama which are highly suitable to work with post-traumatic stress disorder symptoms:

1. and 2. The simple dramatization of traumatic events allows, simultaneously: a) that the client revisits painful facts in a safe environment; and b) to cognitively reprocess what happened, this time without the torpor effect that usually occurs during the trauma.

2. Emotional catharsis helps to drain emotional waste from the traumatic situation.

3. Supplementary reality expands the internal world of the client, adding new actions.

4. Relational work helps prevent frequent isolation in traumatized clients.

5. Sociodrama socializes individual pain, promotes collective actions and the re-signification of traumatic events, in addition to transforming the role of victim into that of survivor.

Blatner, Bouza and Espina Barrio (in KELLERMANN and HUGINS, 2010) highlight the difficulties of mourning (of people, parts of the body, roles prior to the trauma, etc.) in traumatized people. Blatner emphasizes that a person, in a situation of serious loss, lingers between adult states of acceptance of reality and others more regressed and childish, in which they deny and behave as if they could change what happened.

He proposes the "final encounter" technique, a supplementary reality that uses the empty chair: "Let's imagine that this person (or your leg, your group) could come back, and that you could talk to them. What would you say to them?" Three sets of questions can be asked by the director, who should, in the interview, help the client to respond in a detailed, not superficial and vague manner: What did we have in common? What did you mean to me? What did I mean to you?

Bouza & Espina Barrio called attention to anthropological psychodrama, which seeks to recover the rites of passage linked to death (death at home, funeral, exaltation of the dead, crying, etc.). Our Western culture, besides avoiding confrontation with death, offers us collective catastrophes, such as wars, that trivialize the importance of human life.

Marcia Karp (in KELLERMANN and HUGINS, 2010), working with victims of torture and rape, speaks of the importance of a careful, empathic and extremely protective therapist, so as not to retraumatize the victim. In a group session, for example, asking other participants to turn their backs and avoid looking at the embarrassed protagonist.

Her approach prioritizes new visualizations and verbalizations to cognitively and affectionately reprocess the traumatic experience. It seeks to empower the client, giving them control of the traumatic scene and letting them change it as they see fit. Supplementary reality is then used to enact situations in the way the client would like them to occur, and even to experiment if, in fact, it would have been more effective.

Marcia also uses role reversal to finish conversations that did not happen and provide a more complete view of what people thought about the traumatic scene. Finally, her method seeks to restore roles prior to trauma, replaced by the role of the impotent victim, and rekindle the client's hope and power.

Anne Bannister (1997), English psychodramatist and dramaturgist, worked intensely with abused children. In the article "Prisoners of the Family: Psychodrama with Abused Children" (in KELLERMANN and HUGINS, 2010), she evaluates and proves the efficacy of 20 group psychodrama sessions in eliminating post-traumatic stress disorder symptoms. She uses all the technical instruments of psychodrama, emphasizing the mirror technique, for the child to see the scene being interpreted by puppets, role reversal using puppets, using costumes and free interpretation of dramatic vignettes proposed by the children or by the therapist themselves in the style of a "Living Journal" (Moreno, 1973).

Perhaps one of the most creative works, using psychodrama to treat post-traumatic stress disorder, is that of Dr. Kate Hudgins (HUDGINS and TOSCANI, 2013), an American psychologist. She believes that classical psychodrama can retraumatize the client and encourage dissociation. For this reason, she created an experimental model of psychodrama called the Therapeutic Spiral Model (TSM), whose main objective is to ensure safety and containment for trauma survivors.

In the warm-up, she uses what she calls prescriptive roles. They are positive roles which the client highlights and concretizes before starting to work on the traumatic scene. They are three types: roles of restoration; roles of containment; and observation roles.

In dramatization, she uses various security resources: first the protagonist describes the traumatic scene, then watches and witnesses the egos interpreting the scene and, later, he/she interprets his/her role him/herself.

Open-scene dramatization (CUKIER, 1992) is typified according to the level of stress they provide to the client, and the director guides the protagonist in a crescendo of difficulties.

The Containing Double technique is used to prevent dissociation. An auxiliary ego stands next to the protagonist giving them only supportive statements, emphasizing their strengths to confront the traumatic scenes. The "atom role" technique based on the trauma is very interesting and useful, as it shows how the normal roles of the patient's life are overlapped and replaced by others, created by defensive structures and the internalization of the trauma.

Finally, there are many other colleagues who use psychodrama for post-traumatic stress disorder in a creative, dynamic and efficient way. Tyan Dayton (2011), for example, has a model for repairing relational traumas. This author has an entire book of games and technical management for post-traumatic stress groups.

Our foreign colleagues have already realized that we need to gain visibility at the statistical level. This is done by standardizing techniques and their applications, training directors, and designing statistical, quantitative and longitudinal studies.

III.   CONCLUSION AND SUGGESTIONS

Psychodrama has many skilled technical resources to deal with PTSD, many of which have been tested and used in other theoretical approaches, which were able to prove their statistical validity.

We must learn to do the same. My suggestion, after carefully reading the texts written by our foreign colleagues is: 1 - to create a way of therapeutic care that can be statistically tested, without excluding the spontaneity of the therapist and the client, this is our trademark; 2 - group work, collecting cases by pathology and, with the help of statisticians, design longitudinal follow-ups that demonstrate our therapeutic efficacy.

To conclude, I will list some techniques already described and that, admittedly, can help traumatized clients. They are the following:

A)   In the initial interviews:

• Mix empathic listening with gentle questions that create harmony, security and a sense of normality.

• Explain to the client how the human brain works in traumatic situations, to legitimize their symptoms, to create a logic where before there was chaos and to bring hope back. After all, we have already learned from cognitive therapies that changing negative thoughts has the power to change emotional configurations and subsequent behaviors.

- After the verbal interviews, propose the experience of the Social Atom before the trauma and the Social Atom after the trauma, mapping the loss of roles and relationships, and creating an agenda for therapy.

B)   In the warm-up:

- The warm-up must be strategically constructed to mark the client's positive skills, parts in life in which they are strong; and the people, institutions, and spiritual resources that support them. Kate Hudgins has already shown us that this resource protects clients from re-traumatization and dissociations.

C)   In the dramatization:

- Assembly and cognitive-emotional development of the traumatic scene - with successive approximations to the action: first the patient tells, then they watch the scene being played by auxiliary egos; finally they act out the scene. This careful assembly ensures that the warm-up is carried out smoothly, from the superficial to in-depth, from the current to the old. The client controls the drama, modifies the role of the egos, and has the control that was taken from him/her in the original trauma.

- Using role-playing where the client is exposed to the feared or desired scene with all the roles it includes. This is our version of the exposure technique whose efficacy has a strong basis in statistical studies. The exposure starts in our protected clinic, with our supportive presence.

- In the final reparatory stage, seeking the resources that the patient needs to be empowered and perform the necessary mourning work so that the scene, the relationship or the farewell has a dignified closure.

- Using supplementary reality and resistance interpolation to reassure client power. From the somatic psychotherapies, we learned that in the body a defense action was buried by forced submission. Introducing superheroes, fairies and princesses, muscular friends, heroes of humanity can, in a magical moment, unfreeze the oppressed body and surprise the client with a force that he/she thought non-existent.

* Always ending the dramatization with a forward-looking scene and recovery of tasks, roles and social life, which give the client the perception of being a heroic survivor of their own destiny, no longer a passive and impotent victim.

D)   *Sharing*:

* Providing the chance to share experiences that allows the audience, the ego-assistants and the therapist him/herself to share his/her traumatic experiences and include the protagonist in a group of people who, like him/her, survive heroically.

Personally, I have been using Psychodrama with traumatized patients for years. I have written extensively on child abuse, narcissistic and borderline disorders, dissociation, addictions, and I have no doubt about the efficacy of our technique. Over the last ten years, I have been happily following the results of neuroscience that value and validate experiential techniques in psychotherapy. I think this is our time, but we have to do our part!

REFERENCES

BANNISTER, Anne. **The healing drama:** Psychodrama and drama therapy with abused children. London: Jessica Kingsley Publishers, 1997.
BROM, Danny *et al.* **First randomized controlled outcome study on the use of somatic experiencing for PTSD:** preliminary data analysis. 2015. Retrieved   from https://beyondthetraumavortex.wordpress.com/2015/07/22/first-randomized-controlled- outcome-stud.
BRYANT, R. A. Treating acute stress disorder: An evaluation of cognitive behavioural therapy and supporting counseling techniques. **American Journal of Psychiatry**, v.*156*, p. 1780-6, 1999.
BUNMI, O. The cruelest cure? Ethical issues in the implementation of exposure- based treatments. **Cognitive and Behavioral Practice,** v.16, n.2, p. 172-80, 2009.
CARLSON, J. G. *et al.* Eye movement desensitization and reprocessing (EMDR) treatment for combat- related posttraumatic stress disorder. **Journal of Traumatic Stress**, v.11, n.1, p. 3-24, 1998

COHEN, J. A. *et al.* Trauma-focused cognitive behavioral therapy for children and adolescents: An empirical update. **Journal of Interpersonal Violence,** *v. 15, n.11*, p. 1202-23, 2000.

COURTNEY, L. B. *et al.* History of cognitive-behavioral therapy (CBT) in youth. **Child Adolesc Psychiatr Clin. N Am.**, v.20, n.2, p. 179-89, 2011.

CUKIER, Rosa. **Bipersonal psychodrama, its technique, its patient and its therapist**. São Paulo: Editora Ágora, 1992.

CUKIER, Rosa. Foundations of psychodrama: the importance of dramatization. **Brazilian Psychodrama Journal**, v. 12, n.1, p. 143-50, 2004.

DAYTON, T. **Relational trauma repair:** An experiential model for working with PTSD. Interlook. New York: Inc. Publisher, 2011.

ELLIOT, R. *et al.* (1996). A process-experiential approach to post-traumatic stress disorder. In R. Hutter et al. (Eds.), **Client-centered and experiential psychotherapy:** A paradigm in motion. Frankfurt: Lang, 1996.

__________. Process-experiential therapy for posttraumatic stress difficulties. In L. S. GREENBERG *et al.* (Eds.), **Handbook of experiential psychotherapy.** Nova York: Guilford Press, 1998.

HUDGINS, K.; TOSCANI, F. **Healing world trauma with the therapeutic spiral model, psychodramatic stories from the frontlines.** London/Philadelphia: Jessica Kingsley Publishers, 2013.

JONATHAN, I. *et al.* Psychological treatments for chronic post-traumatic stress disorder, systematic review and meta-analysis. **The British Journal of Psychiatry,** *v.190, n.2*, p. 97-104, 2007.

JUDITH, S. B. **Why distinguish between cognitive behavior therapy and cognitive behavior therapy?** Beck Institute for Cognitive Therapy and Research. The Beck Institute Newsletter, 2001.

KELLERMAN, Peter F. (1992). **Focus on psychodrama.** London: Jessica Kingsley Publishers, 1992.

KELLERMAN, P. F.; HUDGINS, M. K. **Psychodrama with trauma survivors:** acting out your pain. MK Books, 2000.

KIPPER, D. A.; RITCHIE, T. The effectiveness of psychodramatic techniques: A meta- analysis. **Group Dynamics Theory Research and Practice** v.7, n.1, p. 13-25, 2003.

LEE, C. W.; CUIJPERS, P. (2015). What does the data say about the importance of eye movement in EMDR? **Journal of Behavior Therapy and Experimental Psychiatry**, v. 45, n.1, 226-8, 2015.

MARKOWITZ, J. C. et al. Is exposure necessary? A randomized clinical trial of interpersonal psychotherapy for PTSD. **Am. Journal of Psychiatry**, v.172, n.5, p. 430-40, 2015.

MCNALLY, R. J. (1999). Research on Eye Movement Desensitization and Reprocessing (EMDR) as a treatment for PTSD. **PTSD Research Quarterly**, v. 10, n.1, p. 1-7, 1999.

MORENO, Jacob Levy. **The Theater of Spontaneity**. São Paulo: Summus, 1923.

OFIR, L. *et al.* Cognitive-Behavioral therapy and psychodynamic psychotherapy in the treatment of combat-related post-traumatic stress disorder: A comparative effectiveness study. **Clinical Psychology & Psychotherapy**, 07, 2015.

PITMAN, R. K. *et al.* Emotional processing during eye movement desensitization and reprocessing therapy of Vietnam veterans with chronic posttraumatic stress disorder. **Compr Psychiatry**, v. 37, n.6, p. 419-29, 1996.

RAUCH, S. A. *et al.* Review of exposure therapy: a gold standard for PTSD treatment. **J Rehabil Res Dev**, v. 49, n.5, p. 679-87, 2012.

RICHARDS, D. A. *et al.* Post-traumatic stress disorder: evaluation of a behavioral treatment program. **Journal of Traumatic Stress**, v. 7, n.4, p. 669-80, 1994.

ULRICH, S. *et al.* Results of psychodynamically oriented trauma – focused inpatient treatment for women with complex posttraumatic stress disorder (PTSD) and borderline personality disorder (BPD). **Bulletin of the Menninger Clinic**, v.70, p. 125-44, 2006.

VAN DER KOLK, Bessel. Beyond the talking cure. Somatic experience and subcortical imprints in the treatment of trauma. In F. SHAPIRO (Ed.), **EMDR and an integrative psychotherapy approach**. Washington, DC: American Psychological Association, p. 57-83, 2002.